THE
BROCKWOOD
vegetarian
COOKBOOK

A collection of recipes
from the School and
Centre by Sue Gerrard
and Raman Patel.

With guest cooks:
Michael Krohnen
Derek Hook

THE BROCKWOOD VEGETARIAN COOKBOOK

KRISHNAMURTI FOUNDATION TRUST

For additional information about the Foundations, Schools
and Study Centres, please write to:

The Krishnamurti Foundation Trust Ltd.,
Brockwood Park, Bramdean,
Hants SO24 0LQ, ENGLAND
Tel: +44(0) 1962 771 525
Fax: +44(0) 1962 771 159
Email: info@brockwood.org.uk
Website: www.brockwood.org.uk
or
Krishnamurti Foundation of America
PO Box 1560, Ojai, CA 93024 - 1560, USA
or
Krishnamurti Foundation India
Vasanta Vihar, 64/5 Greenways Road,
Chennai 600 028, INDIA

Original idea for cover Chris Orr.

Printed by Middleton's Print Works, Ambleside, UK

Contents

Foreword   page 5

The Cooks   page 7

Sue Gerrard   **pages 9 -62**

Talking Recipes   pages 9 - 11

Soups   pages 13 - 20

Main Dishes   pages 23 - 46

Salads & Dressings   pages 47 - 51

Cakes, Cookies & Desserts   pages 53 - 62

Raman Patel   **pages 64 - 112**

Introduction   pages 65 - 67

Complementary Dishes   pages 68 - 80

Main Courses   pages 81 - 97

Desserts   pages 98 - 112

Michael Krohnen   **pages 114 - 131**

Introduction   page 115

Dinner One   pages 116 - 119

Dinner Two   pages 120 - 123

Dinner Three   pages 124 - 127

Dinner Four   pages 128 - 131

Derek Hook   **pages 132 - 141**

Introduction   page 133

Special Occasion Menu   pages 134 - 136

Recipes from Yewfield   pages 137 - 141

Weights & Measures   page 142

Index   pages 143 - 144

Acknowledgements

We would like to acknowledge the kind help and co-operation of staff and students at Brockwood Park for their creativity in producing artwork and photographs. Also thanks are due to Neil and Jane Jinkerson and Ashley Cooper for help with food photography; Maggie Santini for her tireless support in producing this cookbook; and to KLI for making it all possible.

Brockwood Park vegetable garden

Foreword

Since the founding of Brockwood Park by J. Krishnamurti in 1969, thousands of people, including staff members, students and visitors to the Adult Centre and School, have had the pleasure of dining in this remarkable place. For many years now we have had numerous requests to produce a cookbook with the recipes for all those delicious meals from Sue, Raman, Michael, Esme and the many others who have shared their love of fine cuisine and delight in making good food. Special thanks are also due to Alan and Helen Hooker for their help in the early years.

The Krishnamurti Adult Study Centre in Spring.

"In oneself lies the whole world, and if you know how to look and learn, then the door is there and the key is in your hand. Nobody on earth can give you either that key or the door to open, except yourself." J Krishnamurti

Taken from the book You Are The World (page 135).

The Cooks

Sue Gerrard

One of our "founder cooks", along with Esme Carnes and Alan Hooker, Sue now runs the Centre kitchen, Brockwood Park's culinary anchor, what would we do without her! For many years she managed the School kitchen with great warmth and an often needed sense of humour. Her skills as a chef and her ability to handle the "unexpected" are outstanding.

Raman Patel

Came to Brockwood Park in 1979 and worked both in the School and Centre kitchens full-time until 1995. Thrown in at the deep end, he soon displayed a natural gift for cooking and the organisational skills required for running a large kitchen. He became Krishnamurti's personal cook at Brockwood Park. Always popular with the guests, he still cooks at the Centre on a regular basis.

Michael Krohnen

The celebrated chef and author of "The Kitchen Chronicles - 1001 Lunches With Krishnamurti", Michael was Krishnamurti's personal chef in Ojai, California, for many years. He was taught by his good friend, Alan Hooker, owner of the famous California restaurant, The Ranch House. Michael is a regular visiting chef at the School and Centre.

Derek Hook

A vegetarian restaurateur from the Lake District, England, a trustee of both the Krishnamurti School and the Foundation, Derek is a reliable standby when the kitchen needs a helping hand. Along with his culinary delights he brings a jocular and famously punning disposition.

The Brockwood Park Cookbook is a collection of recipes gathered over the years. Vast numbers of people, young and not-so-young, from all corners of the earth, have passed through the school kitchen at Brockwood. Staff, students, visitors: they all start by helping in the kitchen - peeling, chopping, endlessly washing up, and exchanging ideas and recipes. Consequently our food is truly international. In writing this I hope to share with you a little of the experience of being part of "The Kitchen Team".

ESME'S SCONES

These are not the usual white, light variety served with jam and cream in local tea shops. They're substantial, healthy little numbers and were made by the thousand, to be eaten by the multitudes attending the Gatherings. We had a group of hard-working people who used to turn up, year after year, to help feed the thousands of visitors who came to hear the talks. It was estimated that two people could bake ten batches of these scones in a day without completely going mad, that's about 120 per batch. We did this for days beforehand, filling an entire room with them. They were extremely popular and sold well. You see, many of our visitors were not financially well-off (so what's new?) and it was felt that a large wholesome scone with a piece of cheese and apple was affordable, nutritious and filling.

THE ATMOSPHERE

The kitchen atmosphere during the Gatherings was pretty amazing, considering the amount of work it involved. Thousands of loaves of bread were baked by Willy the baker from East Meon. We sliced it all by hand - plenty of muscle and skill was necessary to achieve uniform slices. (If you failed, bread destined for the toaster would burn, or worse, jam up the machine.)

The cheese was also cut by hand. It arrived in blocks of about 40lbs (that's 20kg) and cut with a wire into small blocks before being sliced by hand into two-ounce (50g) portions.

Boxes of fruit were stacked to the ceiling: peaches, nectarines, apples and pears, which all had to be carefully washed and dried before sale.

Whilst my mind is still with the Gatherings, a vast amount of food was needed to feed the multitudes then. Two weeks before each annual event we started cooking curry, pasta sauces, chilli bean stews and so on. We did not have the freezer space to accommodate such quantities, which meant great containers of prepared foods were taken to a Southampton freezer centre to be frozen and stored. We would collect it in an elderly van as required. One day, while travelling along the bypass (no motorway in those days), a large container of chilli beans escaped out of the back door and bounced along the tarmac. Oops! Luckily, no one was hurt, no damage done and the beans were still intact - but can you imagine the headlines if it had turned out differently!

During the holidays I filled the School freezers with quiches, pies, savouries, cakes and desserts to feed the guests, many of whom stayed in the vacated student rooms while others camped in the grounds. The campus was always full to bursting and everyone had to be fed.

DIETS

Anyone who comes to Brockwood is, of course, very aware of diet and more than usually interested and educated about food. This, in many ways, is good, but for the cook it can be something of a nightmare. I have provided for them all: vegans, wheat-free, macrobiotic, anti-Candida, non-dairy, no egg, no onion, no tomato, no sugar. Some are committed vegans, some have serious diet problems and some are merely experimenting... but all have to be fed.

Different dishes ready, one day I actually found myself putting onion rings on top of a plate to distinguish it as a non-onion dish! A large, empty dish saying "WITHOUT" was also served on one occasion - just to make a point.

I must say that most of the recipes in this book can be adapted to suit almost any allergy, food fad, whatever. With the exception of cakes and desserts, those I find most difficult in the absence of such good ingredients as butter and eggs. However, there are books that fill this void.

MISO PIE

This dish is very popular at the School and the Centre. It also freezes very well and is a good standby. It has been adapted from something called "Ricky's Roll". Now I cannot remember who Ricky was, but one day whilst visiting Brockwood he volunteered to cook (and of course we never discourage a keen volunteer). Hence "Ricky's Roll" which consisted of a large sheet of pastry spread with miso and then mushrooms, tomatoes and cheese. After rolling it up and baking, it looked rather like a fat Swiss roll or roulade. When baked it was served in slices. Delicious, but rather heavy with all that pastry, so using the same ingredients I created Miso Pie. Thanks Ricky wherever you are!

LANGUAGE

We've had a lot of fun with languages over the years - I'm ashamed to admit I only speak English (and that with a broad Hampshire accent) and I am full of admiration for those who have several languages to call upon. However, working with multi-lingual people does have its confusing and amusing moments. I cooked for a while with a lovable lady from Russia. She had no English at all and of course my Russian was zero, but we got on pretty well in mime, with frustrations and plenty of hugs and laughter.

One young lady from Holland immortalised scrambled eggs as "scrubbled eggs" which is what they've been called in my house ever since. She also muddled spring greens into "green springs" and why not?

I have heard treacle transmuted into "trickle"; puddings lengthened into "poodings", bowls become "bowels" and rice, of course, is "lice" in some languages. I'm becoming an expert on translating this "International" language. The English, too, have some very strange ways with food: just think of the traditional Christmas Pudding, laden with fruit and heavy ingredients, steamed for up to five hours, stored for months, and then, when needed, served after another two hours of steaming. This takes some explaining to another culture especially an Italian who makes a pasta with sauce in about ten minutes. Once I witnessed a student from Malaysia generously pouring soy sauce over a particularly delicious rice pudding I had just made. Sweet and sour English?

Some students really enjoy being in the kitchen. Others, of course, would do anything to avoid it. Each year seemed to bring one student who was particularly keen on cooking, or who simply liked being in the kitchen. Missing home maybe? We used to have an old Aga stove - always warm and welcoming. It was pretty useless for cooking for large numbers, but it kept the room warm and many secrets and worries were shared leaning on its rail. The hot oven was just the thing to bake potatoes in. Some of you will remember Doris Pratt who in her later years enjoyed a baked potato. In fact we used to pop one into the oven every day for her. In truth I don't think she entirely trusted what might appear for lunch and at least a potato was reliable!

The top of the Aga was excellent for proving bread or making yoghurt and it was a very sad day when the decision had to be made to remove it. The stainless steel hob which stood in its place just didn't seem to have a heart.

I worked in the school kitchen for over twenty years. During this time I had the pleasure of travelling up the hill through this lovely part of Hampshire, past The Lodge gates and into the soft rolling grounds of Brockwood Park, appreciating its beauty in all its seasons for so many years. I have shared in the Brockwood days of many delightful students, staff and visitors. So many memories to treasure. Now at The Centre, where life is more tranquil, the building itself is very beautiful and within its walls a special peace, with time to take a little more care, and the School just across the south lawn. Paradise did someone say? Well almost, I am indeed a very fortunate woman.

Sue Gerrard

SOUPS
••••••••••••

Beetroot Soup

Carrot and Leek Soup

Carrot Soup

Celeriac Soup

Chickpea with Rosemary Soup

Fresh Pea Soup

Leek Soup

Dahl Soup

Lentil Soup

Mushroom Soup

Pumpkin Soup

Watercress Soup

Split Pea Soup

Beetroot Soup

1 tablespoon olive oil or 2 oz (50g) butter
1 large onion, chopped
1 large potato, peeled and chopped
1 lb (450g) raw beetroot, peeled and chopped
2 heaped teaspoons bouillon powder or vegetable stock cube
1/4 teaspoon ground cloves
salt and pepper
1 1/2 pts (800ml) hot water
little pouring cream to finish if desired

In a large saucepan, heat the olive oil or butter. Add the onion and cook for a while, followed by the potato and beetroot, stir around and cook some more, add the bouillon powder and ground cloves, pour on the water, bring to the boil, cover and simmer until you are sure the beetroot is soft. Blend the soup, taste and season as necessary with salt and pepper.

A swirl of cream on serving gives the finishing touch to the beautiful appearance of the soup.

Carrot and Leek Soup

1 1/2 oz (40g) butter or a little olive oil
1 onion finely chopped
1 medium size potato finely chopped
1 large carrot finely chopped
2 large leeks finely chopped
2 pts (1.5 ltr) hot water
1 tablespoon dried dill weed or fresh if available
2 teaspoons bouillon powder or a vegetable stock cube
salt and pepper

In a large saucepan melt butter or heat oil, add onion and sauté, add potato and carrot and cook for a few minutes, then add hot water and bouillon or stock cube, bring to the boil and simmer until vegetables are soft, then add leeks and return to the boil, reduce heat and continue to simmer until leeks are cooked but have retained their colour.

Season to taste with salt and pepper.

Carrot Soup

Serves 4

1$\frac{1}{2}$ oz (40g) butter or 1 tablespoon olive oil
1 large onion chopped
1 lb (450g) prepared carrot, chopped
1 large potato sliced
1$\frac{1}{2}$ pts (800ml) hot water
2 teaspoons bouillon powder or vegetable stock cube
$\frac{1}{4}$ whole nutmeg grated
salt and pepper
some freshly chopped parsley to garnish
a little milk or cream if desired

In a medium saucepan melt the butter or heat the oil, add the onions and sauté gently for a while, add the potato and carrot, toss around for a few minutes and continue cooking. Then pour on the water with the bouillon powder or stock cube, grated nutmeg and bring to simmering point, cover pan and cook until the vegetables are very soft. This will take approximately 1 hour depending on the size of the vegetable pieces. Remove from the heat and blend together until smooth, season with salt and pepper, perhaps a little more water if consistency too thick, or if you prefer a little milk or cream to round off the flavour. Garnish with parsley and serve.

Celeriac Soup

Serves 4

2 oz (50g) butter
1 onion roughly chopped
1 lb (450g) prepared celeriac roughly chopped
4 stalks celery roughly chopped
1 medium potato roughly chopped
1$\frac{3}{4}$ pts (1ltr) water
2 teaspoons bouillon powder or vegetable stock cube
a little milk
salt and black pepper
freshly chopped parsley

In a large pan, melt the butter, add the onion and cook for a while, do not brown. Add the celeriac, celery and potato and let them sweat for a while stirring around. Pour on the water with bouillon or stock cube, bring to the boil and simmer until all the vegetables are very soft, blend, season with salt and pepper and add a little milk to make to the required consistency. Garnish with freshly chopped parsley and serve.

Chickpea with rosemary soup   *Serves 4*

8 oz (225g) chickpeas (dry weight)
tablespoon olive oil
1 clove garlic crushed
1 large onion roughly chopped
1 heaped tablespoon fresh rosemary crushed and finely chopped
zest and juice of 1 lemon
salt and pepper
water

Place soaked chickpeas with the rosemary in a large saucepan, cover generously with plenty of water and cook until very tender. When cooked, drain, reserving the stock. Measure the stock to $1^3/4$ pts (1 ltr) making up with extra water if necessary.

Heat oil in a medium pan, add onions and garlic and cook until soft. Add the chickpeas with the rosemary stock, lemon juice and zest. Bring to the boil and simmer for about 15 minutes. Liquidise or blend until smooth, seasoning to taste with salt and pepper.

Fresh Pea Soup   *Serves 4*

2 tablespoons olive oil or 2 oz (50g) butter
1 large onion roughly chopped
1 large potato roughly chopped
12 oz (350g) fresh or frozen peas
$1^3/4$ pts (1 ltr) water or light stock
generous handful of fresh mint chopped
salt and black pepper to taste
little milk or cream if desired

In a large saucepan melt the butter or heat the oil, add the onion and sauté for a few minutes but do not brown. Add the potato and water, bring to the boil and simmer until onions and potato are soft. Add the mint and peas, return to boil and simmer until the peas are cooked but not discoloured. Blend and season with salt and pepper. A little milk or cream may be added to round off the soup which should result in a beautiful bright green colour.

Serve hot or chilled.

Leek Soup

2 oz (50g) butter or 2 tablespoons olive oil
1 onion finely chopped
1 large potato chopped
3 leeks finely chopped
1³/4 pts (1 ltr) water
2 teaspoons bouillon powder or vegetable stock cube
black pepper
salt

In a medium saucepan melt butter or heat oil, add onion and sauté until tender, then add the potato with the water and bouillon powder or stock cube, bring to the boil and simmer until the potato is soft. Add the finely chopped leeks and cook for a little longer until they are tender but retaining their colour. Season to taste with pepper and salt and serve.

Dahl Soup

3 tablespoons vegetable oil
6 oz (175g) red split lentils
approx 1³/4 pts (1 ltr) water
approx 14 oz (400g) can chopped tomatoes
1 large onion finely chopped
1 tablespoon black mustard seeds
1 teaspoon turmeric powder
1 heaped teaspoon medium curry powder
salt
juice ¹/2 lemon
handful of fresh chopped coriander

Rinse lentils and place in medium saucepan with water, bring to the boil and simmer until lentils are well cooked. It is quite a good idea to blend the dahl at this stage to make it smooth, but not necessary.

Meanwhile in a separate pan heat the oil until it is very hot, throw in the mustard seeds. If the oil is hot they should jump and pop, then immediately add the chopped onion and reduce heat. The onion should not brown or burn. Cook until onion soft, then add the turmeric powder and curry powder and cook for a moment or two. Pour on the dahl, add the tinned tomatoes, lemon juice and season well with salt. Food with Indian flavours needs a surprising amount of salt. If soup is too thick add more water. Finally garnish with fresh coriander and serve.

Lentil Soup

2 tablespoons olive oil
6 oz (175g) whole brown lentils (dry weight) and then cooked
1 onion chopped
1 small carrot chopped
1 courgette chopped
2 oz (50g) mushrooms chopped
$1/4$ red pepper chopped
1 can chopped tomatoes approx 14 oz (400g)
approx 1 pt (570ml) water
2 teaspoons vecon stock or a vegetable stock cube & $1/4$ teaspoon marmite
black pepper and salt to taste if needed
handful of fresh coriander chopped

In a medium pan heat the oil, add the onions and cook for a few minutes. Add the remaining vegetables and coriander and cook for a few more minutes. Finally add the tomatoes, Vecon or stock cube and marmite with the cooked lentils and water, bring to the boil and simmer until vegetables are soft, season with pepper and salt as necessary. Serve.

Mushroom Soup

2 oz (50g) butter
6 oz (175g) mushrooms, sliced
$1^1/2$ oz (40g) plain white flour
$1^3/4$ pts (1ltr) vegetable stock or water flavoured with bouillon powder
little cream or milk
black pepper

Melt the butter in a medium pan, add the mushrooms and sauté for a while until soft, then add the flour while stirring, followed by the stock, still stirring. Bring to the boil and simmer for a couple of minutes. Add the cream or milk and season with pepper according to taste. Serve.

Pumpkin Soup

Serves 4

1$\frac{1}{2}$ oz (40g) butter or 1 tablespoon olive oil
1 large onion chopped
1 lb (700g) prepared pumpkin cut into chunks
1 medium potato cut into slices
2 teaspoons bouillon powder or a vegetable stock cube
salt and black pepper
approx $\frac{3}{4}$ pt (425 ml) hot water
finely chopped parsley to garnish
a little milk or cream if desired

In a medium saucepan melt the butter or heat the oil, add the onions and sauté gently for a while, add the potato and pumpkin, toss around for a few minutes still cooking, then pour on the water with the bouillon powder or stock cube, bring to simmering point, cover and cook until the vegetables are very soft. This will take approx 1 hour depending on size of the vegetable pieces and age of the pumpkin. Remove from the heat, blend together until smooth, season with salt and pepper, perhaps a little more water if too thick, or if you prefer a little milk or cream. Garnish with parsley and serve.

Watercress Soup

Serves 6

2 oz (50g) butter
1 large onion roughly chopped
2 large potatoes, peeled and roughly chopped
2 pts (1$\frac{1}{2}$ ltrs) water or light vegetable stock
4 bunches watercress, roughly chopped
$\frac{1}{4}$ pt (150 ml) double cream
salt and black pepper

In a large saucepan, melt the butter, add the onion and cook until soft but not coloured, add the potatoes and stir. Pour on the water, bring to the boil and simmer until the onions and potatoes are soft then add the watercress, return to the boil and cook for a few minutes until the watercress has softened. Do not overcook or the brilliant green colour of this soup will be lost. Blend until very smooth, season well with salt and black pepper. Stir in the cream and serve.

This soup is very popular with our Centre Guests. Watercress is grown locally at Alresford and Warnford.

Split Pea Soup

3 tablespoons vegetable oil
7 oz (200g) split peas, green or yellow,
1 large onion chopped
2 large carrots diced
3 sticks celery chopped
12 oz (350g) can chopped tomatoes (approx)
2 teaspoons cumin powder
2 teaspoons coriander powder
good pinch ground cloves
a squeeze of lemon
salt and pepper

Split peas should be soaked overnight, then rinsed, placed in a large saucepan and covered with plenty of water, bring them to the boil and simmer until soft. Add the can of tomatoes and blend until smooth, return to the pan.

In a large frying pan or saucepan, heat the oil, add the onions and celery then sauté until soft. Add the dry spices and cook a little more, then add this mixture to the blended split peas and tomatoes in the saucepan. Bring to simmer. You may need a little more water to achieve the required consistency, season with salt and pepper and lemon juice and serve.

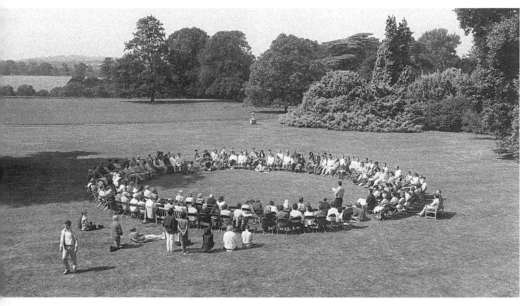

A quiet meeting on the front lawn at Brockwood.

Esme NOT making scones in the early seventies.

MAIN DISHES

Bean Cakes

Butterbean Casserole

Butterbean or Tofu Stroganoff

Corn Savoury

Filled Tomatoes

Kalyani Rice

Leek Croustade

Lentil Rissoles

Moussaka

Mushroom Nut Roast with Spicy Peanut Sauce

Mushroom Pancakes

Shepherds Pie

Tandoori Bean Cakes

Tofu with Tarragon and Mushroom Sauce

Spinach Rice Bake

Spicy Vegetables & Chickpeas with Couscous

PASTRY DISHES

Broccoli Flan

Carrot Flan with Potato Peanut Pastry

Miso Pie

Onion Tart

Spinach Pie

Vegetable Cobbler

Winter Vegetable Pie

Bean Cakes

4 oz (110g) black eye beans
4 oz (110g) green lentils
1 pint (570ml) water
1 bay leaf
2 teaspoons dried thyme
1 tablespoon olive oil
1 medium onion, finely chopped
1 medium carrot, grated
1 small red pepper, cut into fine dice
pinch chilli powder
1 clove garlic, crushed
1/4 teaspoon grated nutmeg
1 tablespoon tomato paste
2 tablespoons whole-wheat flour
olive oil for frying
salt and black pepper

Beans should be soaked over night and drained, lentils do not need soaking.

Place beans and lentils in a medium pan and cover with 1 pint of water. Add bay leaf and thyme, bring to the boil and simmer for abut 45 minutes until beans and lentils are soft and all the water is absorbed. If there is any liquid remaining, drain in a colander. Remove bay leaf. Now they should be mashed with a fork and seasoned well with salt and black pepper. Cover with a cloth to avoid drying and set aside.

Take a large frying pan over a medium flame, add olive oil and the onion, carrot, pepper, garlic and chilli powder and sauté for a few minutes until softened. Add this to the mashed beans and lentils with the tomato paste and nutmeg, mix well and then with dampened hands shape the mixture into 12 round bean cakes. Place them on a plate, cover with cling film and store them in a refrigerator until needed.

When ready to serve coat lightly with seasoned flour and fry in olive oil until golden on both sides. Drain, garnish with parsley or watercress.

Serve with a good helping of fried onions and creamed potatoes.

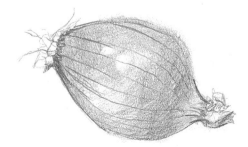

Butterbean Casserole

2 tablespoons olive oil
7 oz (200g) butterbeans
1 onion chopped
1 clove garlic crushed
bay leaf
2 carrots cut into chunks
3 sticks celery cut into chunks
1 red pepper cut into large dice
8 oz (225g) shallots
6 oz (175g) button mushrooms
2 teaspoons tomato paste
good pinch dried thyme and sage
2 teaspoons bouillon powder or vegetable stock cube
black pepper and salt to taste

Soak butterbeans overnight. Place in saucepan and cover with water, bring to the boil, cook for a few minutes, drain, throw away the water, cover again with plenty of water, add bouillon powder or stock cube and bay leaf. Bring to the boil and simmer gently until just cooked. Leave whole. Drain, reserving the stock.

Heat the olive oil in a large saucepan, add the shallots and sauté for a while until coloured a golden brown, remove shallots from pan and set aside. Put the chopped onions in the pan and sauté until golden brown, add the garlic and the other vegetables and sauté for 5 minutes, add sage and thyme, pour over reserved stock from beans, stir in the tomato paste, add a little water if necessary, the vegetables should be covered in liquid but not swimming. Cover and simmer until vegetables almost cooked, then add the shallots and butter beans, simmer until all cooked, season with salt and pepper to taste.

Serve with creamed or roast potatoes and a green vegetable.

Butterbean or Tofu Stroganoff

2 cloves garlic crushed

1 large onion chopped

4 oz (110g) firm white mushrooms, sliced

7 oz (200g) cauliflower, small florets

7 oz (200g) broccoli, small florets

4 oz (110g), dry weight, butterbeans, soaked overnight and cooked

or

8 oz (225g) firm tofu cut into cubes

1 can chopped tomatoes (approx 12 oz (400g) can)

$^1/_2$ pt (300ml) full cream milk

3 oz (75g) butter

$^1/_4$ teaspoon ground black pepper

2 teaspoons medium curry powder

salt to taste

In a large saucepan, melt the butter, slowly cook the onion and garlic until well cooked and soft but not browned. Add tomatoes and simmer for a while. Add pepper, curry powder and salt, simmer a little more adding milk. Remove from heat and blend until sauce is smooth. Return to heat, add sliced mushrooms and cooked butter beans or tofu, stir carefully until heated through. Meanwhile, steam broccoli and cauliflower until just tender and stir into sauce over very gentle heat.

Serve with rice of your choice.

To make this dish vegan, substitute butter with margarine and milk with soya milk.

Corn Savoury

2 oz (50g) butter
1 onion, chopped
2 teaspoons dried basil
$^1/_2$ red pepper, chopped
$^1/_2$ green pepper, chopped
1 can sweetcorn, approx 12 oz (340g) drained
4 oz (110g) grated Cheddar cheese
3 large eggs, beaten
salt and pepper

In a medium pan, melt the butter, add the onion with the basil and cook gently until the onions are soft and golden. Add the peppers and continue to cook until peppers are softened. Remove from heat, stir in the sweetcorn, grated cheese and beaten eggs, season with salt and pepper. Pour into a buttered oven proof dish approx 7 inches x 9 inches (18cm x 23cm) bake at 160°c for about 30 minutes until set and golden.

Serve with baked potatoes and green vegetable.

Filled Tomatoes

In a measuring jug put rice to come up to the $^1/_2$ pt (275ml) mark

2 oz (50g) whole brown lentils cooked until tender

2 tablespoons olive oil

2 onions finely chopped

8 oz (225g) mushrooms finely chopped

12 large tomatoes

4 oz (110g) cheddar cheese grated

2 tablespoons capers

little soy sauce

salt and black pepper

handful of chopped parsley

Cook rice in the usual way in double the volume of water. A little bouillon powder added to the water will help with the final flavour. Slice the tops off each tomato and scoop out the middle, making it hollow. You will not need the tops or the flesh although they can be used for soup. Place the tomatoes in a shallow oven proof dish and season with salt and pepper or herb salt.

Heat oil in a medium pan, add the onions and cook gently for a few minutes, add the mushrooms and sauté with the onions until they have taken on a little colour. Remove from heat.

In a large mixing bowl, place the cooked rice with the cooked mushrooms and onions, lentils, capers, season with soy sauce, salt and pepper and add most of the parsley. Pile the mixture into the prepared tomatoes, cover each one with grated cheese. Bake at 170°c for 20 mins until tomatoes are tender and cheese melted. Scatter remaining parsley on top and serve.

Any long grain rice will be suitable for this dish. Quinoa works very well in place of rice.

Broccoli and carrots would be a good side dish.

Kalyani Rice

This is a delicious way of using up left over cooked rice and vegetables. It takes its name from the Indian lady who introduced us to it.

Quantities are, of course, variable depending on the amount of 'left overs'. However, we have assumed that you have approx 500g cooked rice and 250g cooked vegetables.

> 2 fl oz (55ml) vegetable oil
> 2 medium onions sliced
> 3 tomatoes chopped
> 1 teaspoon black mustard seeds
> 1 small whole red chilli
> 1 teaspoon turmeric powder
> 1 teaspoon ground cumin powder
> 1 teaspoon ground coriander powder
> salt
> lemon juice
> fresh coriander

Heat oil in a large pan. When the oil is very hot (but not smoking) throw in the mustard seeds, they should jump and pop, immediately add chopped onions and reduce heat. Cook for a few minutes. Add dry spices, some salt and the tomatoes and simmer gently for about 10 minutes. Stir in the vegetables and rice, heat through.

Before serving add lemon juice, to taste, possibly more salt and sprinkle with fresh chopped coriander.

It is most important, as in reheating any food, to make sure that the rice and vegetables are very hot. Also that the 'left overs' you are reheating were previously cooled quickly and kept in a refrigerator. Do not attempt to reheat Kalyani.

This quantity would serve about 4 for a supper dish, depending on appetites. The addition of a few cooked lentils, or toasted nuts would add protein if Kalyani is served alone.

Leek Croustade

Crust
1 clove garlic
4 oz (110g) fresh breadcrumbs
3 oz (75g) butter
3 oz (75g) nuts of your choice, finely chopped
4 oz (110g) grated cheddar cheese
1 heaped teaspoon mixed dried herbs
pinch of salt and pepper

Filling
$1/2$ pt (300ml) milk
2 oz (50g) butter
1 oz (25g) plain white flour
1 tablespoon fresh parsley chopped
3 large leeks, chopped & steamed until tender, then well drain
1 can chopped tomatoes, 14 oz (400g) juice not required
Nutmeg, salt and pepper

Crust

In a medium pan, melt the butter and add garlic. Remove from the heat. Stir in all the remaining ingredients and mix well. Oil a shallow pie dish, approximately 8" x 10" (20cm x 25cm). Take $1/3$ of the crust mix and pat it into the pie dish to line the base and sides. Bake at 170°c for about 10 minutes.

Meanwhile, make the filling

In a medium pan, melt the butter, stir in the flour then slowly add the milk, stirring or whisking until a thick smooth sauce is made. Remove from the heat. Stir in the tomatoes, leeks and parsley. Season with nutmeg, salt and pepper to taste.

Spoon the mixture into the baked pie crust, spread remaining crust on the top and return to the oven for about 10 to 15 minutes until golden.

New potatoes and carrots would go well with this dish.

Lentil Rissoles

 2 tablespoons vegetable oil
 1 large onion, finely chopped
 2 sticks celery, finely chopped
 1 large carrot, finely chopped
 8 oz (225g) continental lentils (green)
 1pt (570ml) water
 1 teaspoon ground coriander
 salt and pepper
 handful chopped fresh parsley
 6 oz (175g) whole-wheat breadcrumbs
 little whole-wheat flour
 1 egg, beaten
 oil for shallow frying.

Heat the oil in a large saucepan, add onion, celery and carrot and sauté until softened. Add the lentils, water, coriander, little salt and pepper, bring to the boil and simmer gently for about an hour until lentils are cooked and water absorbed. Remove from the heat and mix in the parsley and one third of the breadcrumbs. Turn into a dish and leave to cool.

When cool, shape the mixture into rissoles, coat with flour, dip into beaten egg and coat with remaining breadcrumbs.

Pour oil into a frying pan, when hot, add rissoles and fry until golden on both sides.

Serve with tomato sauce. Any form of potatoes or rice would be good with these rissoles. Also serve with a green vegetable.

Lunchtime at the centre.

Moussaka

olive oil
2 onions, chopped
1 clove garlic, chopped
1 teaspoon dried basil
12 oz (350g) mushrooms, sliced
3 sticks celery, chopped
9 oz (250g) pack of Quorn or 9 oz (250g) cooked whole brown lentils
2 aubergines approx 1 lb (450g)
can chopped tomatoes approx $1^1/4$ 1b (600g)
1 tablespoon tomato paste
1 oz (25g) butter
1 oz (25g) plain white flour
$^1/2$ pt (275ml) milk
2 large eggs, beaten
nutmeg, salt and black pepper
3 oz (75g) cheddar cheese, grated

Slice aubergines and place in a colander. Sprinkle with salt, cover with a plate and set aside.

In a large pan, heat 2 tablespoons of olive oil then add the onions, garlic and celery with the basil and cook for a while until golden. Add the mushrooms and cook a little longer. Add the Quorn or lentils, stir in the tomato paste and the canned tomatoes and continue to cook for a few more minutes. Season to taste with salt and pepper. Mixture should be a very thick sauce. If it appears thin, increase heat until liquid has evaporated.

Next the aubergines. Push the plate down on the aubergines so that the liquid from them drains away. Take a large frying pan, pour in some olive oil, heat and fry them off, as they are cooked place on kitchen towel to absorb the excess oil. Take a baking dish approx 8 inches x 11 inches (20cm x 29cm) and line the base with half of the aubergine. Cover with the Quorn/lentil mixture, then arrange remaining aubergine on the top.

In a small saucepan, melt the butter, add the flour, stir in the milk to make a sauce, season with nutmeg, salt and pepper. Remove from heat and stir in beaten egg. Pour over the aubergines, sprinkle with grated cheese and bake at 160°c for approx 40 mins until golden and set.

Serve with crusty granary bread and a green salad.

Mushroom Nut Roast
with Spicy Peanut Sauce

Serves 4

2 fl oz (55ml) sunflower oil
2 medium onions, finely chopped
4 oz (110g) whole-wheat breadcrumbs
4 oz (110g) nuts of your choice, finely chopped
8 oz (220g) mushrooms, finely chopped
1 teaspoon yeast extract mixed into 4 fl oz (110ml) hot water
1 heaped teaspoon dried mixed herbs
handful of fresh chopped parsley
salt and black pepper
1 egg, beaten
few flaked almonds

Sauce
1 tablespoon sunflower oil
1 small onion very finely chopped
1 can tomatoes approx 13 oz (400g)
1 tablespoon peanut butter (crunchy or smooth)
good pinch of chilli powder
salt to taste
water

In a large saucepan, heat the oil and cook the onions for a while until softened before adding the mushrooms, then cook until soft. Remove from the heat. Add all the other ingredients with the exception of the flaked almonds. Mix well and season with salt and pepper. Oil and line a small loaf tin with non-stick baking parchment and sprinkle a few flaked almonds in the base. Place the nut roast mixture in the tin, smooth out and bake for approx 30 minutes at 170°c. Remove from the oven, leave to rest for a few minutes, then turn out onto a serving plate, almonds uppermost. Serve sliced and hot with spicy peanut sauce, creamed potatoes and a green vegetable. Alternatively serve cold without the sauce accompanied by salads or as a sandwich filler.

Sauce

In a small saucepan, heat the oil, add the onion and cook until soft. Add the tomatoes, peanut butter and chilli and cook for a while, then blend, seasoning with salt and sufficient water to make a pouring sauce.

Pancakes
4 oz (110g) plain flour
pinch salt
2 eggs
7 fl oz (200ml) milk mixed together with 3 fl oz (75ml) water
2 oz (50g) butter, melted
oil for cooking

Sieve the flour and salt into a mixing bowl, making a well in the centre. Break eggs into the well and start whisking (electric or manual, it makes no difference), gradually drawing in the flour from the sides of the well as you whisk till all the flour is incorporated and the mixture is a smooth, thin batter. Heat a small omelette pan approx 6 inches (15cm) diameter. Lightly oil the pan and spoon in some of the batter swirling to cover the base very thinly, approx 1-2 tablespoons of batter should make one pancake. When it is cooked on one side flip it over and cook on the other side, the   procedure is very fast, have a warm plate at hand to slide the cooked pancakes on as they are cooked. This amount of mixture should make 12-14 pancakes.

Filling
2 oz (50g) butter
3lbs (1.35kg) mushrooms, finely chopped
2 cloves garlic, crushed
2 oz (50g) plain white flour
3/4 pt milk
salt and black pepper and a good grating of nutmeg
handful of chopped parsley
a little extra milk

Melt the butter in a large saucepan. Add mushrooms with garlic and cook until tender and any water evaporates. Stir in the flour followed by the milk, stir well and continue to cook. The mixture will become very thick. Season well with salt, pepper and nutmeg. Add parsley. Remove from the heat.

Now put a spoonful of the mushroom filling onto each pancake, roll it up and place in a shallow oven proof dish, reserving approx one quarter of the mixture. When ready to serve, place the dish of filled pancakes into the oven at 160°c to heat through (time will depend on how cold the pancakes have become.) In the meantime heat the remaining mushroom mixture, adding a little milk to make a pouring sauce. When the dish is hot, pour along the centre of the pancakes, sprinkle with little more chopped parsley and serve.

Serve with chunky carrots and green beans.

Shepherds Pie

2 tablespoons olive oil
4 oz (110g) green lentils
1 large onion, chopped
4 sticks celery, chopped
4 medium carrots, chopped
can chopped tomatoes approx 14 oz (400g)
2 bay leaves
good pinch dried thyme and sage
salt and pepper

Wash lentils, cover with water and cook until tender. Drain, reserving stock. In a large frying pan, heat the oil, add the onion and sauté until golden. Add the celery, carrots, bay leaves, thyme and sage and continue to cook gently. This procedure should not be hurried, let the vegetables sweat and brown a little. When they are soft add the can of tomatoes, lentils and sufficient stock to make a stiff sauce. Season with salt and pepper to taste and pour into an 8 inch x 9 inch (20cm x 23cm) baking dish.

Topping
4 large potatoes
2 oz (50g) butter
little milk
nutmeg
salt and pepper
a little vegetable oil

Boil the potatoes in water until soft, drain and mash. Add the butter, season with nutmeg, salt and pepper to taste, beat with a fork, adding sufficient milk to achieve a soft creamy consistency. Spread this over the top of the lentils, forking a pattern. Finally drizzle a little vegetable oil over the top which will help the finished dish to be golden brown. Place in a preheated oven 180°c for approx 45 minutes until potato is crisp and golden.

Serve with broccoli, spring greens or green beans.

Tandoori Bean Cakes

8 oz (225g) dried pinto beans or red kidney beans
I tablespoon vegetable oil
1 onion, finely chopped
2 cloves garlic, crushed
2 teaspoons tandoori spice or a mixture of your own Indian spices
2 teaspoon ground cumin
$1^{1}/4$ oz (40g) whole-wheat breadcrumbs
2 tablespoons fresh chopped coriander
2 tablespoons tomato paste
3 oz (75g) carrot, finely grated
salt and black pepper
3 tablespoons whole-wheat flour
1 teaspoon paprika

Yoghurt sauce
$1/4$ pt (150ml) plain yoghurt
1 tablespoon tomato ketchup
lemon juice
little salt

Beans should be soaked overnight and then covered with plenty of fresh water and brought to the boil. Boil rapidly for 10 minutes then drain. Add fresh water and cook until tender. In a sauté pan heat the oil and add the onion and garlic. Cook until soft then add spices and cook for a further minute or two. Place cooked beans, onions, breadcrumbs, tomato paste, carrot and coriander into a food processor or blender, season with salt and pepper and blend until well mixed and fairly smooth. Turn mixture out into a bowl.

Mix together the flour and paprika on a plate. With dampened hands divide the blended bean mixture into 8 balls (more if you want to make smaller bean cakes). Flatten and shape up and coat with the flour paprika mix. When ready the bean cakes may be brushed with oil and grilled or fried in a little oil until golden and crisp.

Serve hot with cold yoghurt sauce. To make the sauce simply mix the ingredients together using lemon juice and salt to taste.

Serve with a mixture of rice and finely cut green beans and red peppers.

Tofu with Tarragon and Mushroom Sauce   *Serves 4*

a little olive oil

8 oz (225g) firm white mushrooms, sliced

1 red pepper, diced

2 cloves garlic, crushed

2 teaspoons dried tarragon or 1 tablespoon of fresh

handful of chopped parsley

2 oz (50g) butter

1 oz (25g) plain white flour

3/4 pt (425ml) milk

8 oz (225g) firm tofu, cubed

salt and black pepper to taste

Heat pan. Add small amount of olive oil, sauté mushrooms, pepper and garlic until just softened. Do not brown or overcook.

Meanwhile in a separate pan, melt butter, stir in flour, add milk gradually over a slow heat, stirring or whisking until the sauce is smooth and creamy. Add the tarragon and cook for a few minutes, then add the mushroom pepper mix, stir in the parsley and season well. Lastly sir in the tofu taking care not to break it up. Heat through.

Serve immediately with brown rice. Cooked green peas and diced carrot mixed in with the rice would create a simple and colourful dish.

Spinach Rice Bake

a little vegetable oil
1 large onion, finely chopped
12 oz (300g) rice. Cook in double the amount of water as usual
1 lb 8 oz (700g) spinach, lightly steamed and chopped
4 oz (110g) cottage cheese
2 oz (50g) cheddar cheese, grated
2 eggs, beaten
1/2 teaspoon dried sage
1/2 whole nutmeg, grated
salt and pepper
few sunflower seeds

In a large pan, heat oil and sauté chopped onion until soft and golden. Remove from heat. Add cooked rice and spinach, mix well, add cottage cheese. Season with sage, nutmeg, salt and pepper. Take care with sage, too much can overpower the dish. Taste to check seasoning. Add beaten eggs and mix well. Place in a baking dish and finish with grated cheddar cheese and a sprinkling of sunflower seeds.

Bake at 160°c for approx 30 - 40 minutes.

Serve hot with a side vegetable of your choice. Carrots look and taste well with this dish.

Alan Rowlands, Professor of Piano, composes himself before lunch.

Spicy Vegetables & Chickpeas with Couscous

Serves 6

olive oil
1 clove garlic, crushed
1 large onion
2 medium carrots
2 medium courgettes
1 red pepper
1 green pepper
2 sticks celery
2 small potatoes
(all vegetables should be cut into large chunks)
2 lb (900g) fresh tomatoes, chopped
7 oz (250g) dry weight chick peas soaked overnight, cooked, stock reserved
1 teaspoon turmeric powder
1 teaspoon ground cumin
1 teaspoon ground coriander
1 small whole chilli, or good pinch of chilli powder
salt and pepper to taste
fresh chopped coriander

Pour a generous amount of olive oil into a large pan and heat. Add the onions and garlic and cook for a few minutes, add all the other vegetables and cook a little more adding the spices. Stir in the cooked chickpeas with a little of the reserved stock, reduce heat and simmer very slowly until all the vegetables are cooked but remain in shape. This should take approx 30 minutes depending on the size of the vegetables. Dish improves if left standing for a while, reheat on serving. Garnish with fresh chopped coriander.

Couscous

12 oz (350g) couscous
$1/2$ teaspoon salt
little olive oil
$1^1/2$ volume boiling water

Place couscous in a pan with salt, stir in a little olive oil to coat the grains, pour on boiling water, cover and leave to stand for 10 minutes. Fluff up with a fork and serve.

pastry
4 oz (110g) plain flour
2 oz (50g) butter
pinch of salt and pepper
water to mix

filling
1^1/$_2$ tablespoons tomato ketchup
8 oz (225g) broccoli cut into small florets, steamed until tender & drained well
1^1/$_2$ oz (40g) butter
1^1/$_2$ oz (40g) plain flour
10fl oz (275ml) milk
4 oz (110g) cheddar cheese, grated
salt and pepper
nutmeg
2 eggs, beaten

Place flour, butter and a pinch of salt and pepper into a mixing bowl and rub together until mixture resembles fine breadcrumbs. Mix together with a little water until dough comes into a ball. Roll out on a floured surface and line an 8 inch (20cm) oiled flan dish. Bake at 180°c for 15 minutes. Before baking it is best to line the pastry shell with greaseproof paper and fill with baking beans so that it keeps its shape.

In a small saucepan melt the butter, add flour and mix well, stir in the milk and stir until a smooth sauce results. Season with salt and pepper and grated nutmeg. Remove from heat and stir in three quarters of the cheese and the two beaten eggs.

When pastry shell is cooked, spread base with tomato ketchup, arrange broccoli on top, pour over the sauce, sprinkle with grated cheese and return to the oven for about 20 - 30 minutes until set and golden.

Carrot Flan with Potato Peanut Pastry *Serves 4*

pastry
4 oz (110g) mashed potato
2 oz (50g) butter
5 oz (150g) whole-wheat flour
1 teaspoon baking powder
2 oz (50g) crunchy peanut butter
good pinch salt
water to mix

filling
1 oz (25g) butter
1 medium onion, very finely chopped
1 oz (25g) plain white flour
$1/4$ pint (150ml) milk
3 oz (75g) grated raw potato
8 oz (225g) grated raw carrot
3 oz (75g) grated mature cheddar cheese
$1/2$ teaspoon dried thyme
good pinch of freshly grated nutmeg
1 teaspoon soy sauce
salt and pepper
2 large eggs, beaten

To make the pastry, place mashed potato, butter, flour, baking powder, salt and peanut butter in a large mixing bowl and rub together. Mix with a little water to make a firm dough. Turn onto a floured surface and roll out to line a large buttered flan dish approx 8 inches (20cm) in diameter.

In a medium pan, melt the butter, add the onion and cook until soft. Add the flour followed by the milk and cook to make a thick sauce. Then add the grated potatoes, carrots, thyme, nutmeg, soy sauce and half of the grated cheese, season with salt and pepper. Continue to cook gently for a few minutes, stirring constantly. Remove from the heat, stir in the beaten eggs and pour into the pastry case. Sprinkle with remaining cheese and bake for approx 45 minutes at 150°c until golden.

Serve hot with broccoli and buttered parsnips. Alternatively cold with salad.

Miso Pie

pastry
8 oz (225g) plain flour, white or whole-wheat or a mix of both
4 oz (125g) butter or margarine, butter cut into small pieces
pinch of salt and cayenne pepper
water to mix

filling
a little vegetable oil
1 large onion, chopped
8 oz (225g) mushrooms, thinly sliced
2 ripe tomatoes, skinned and sliced
3 oz (75g) cheddar cheese, grated
1 tablespoon miso mixed together with 1 tablespoon water to make paste
little milk or egg to finish

Place flour, salt, cayenne pepper and butter or margarine into a large mixing bowl and rub together until the mixture resembles fine breadcrumbs. Add a little water, sufficient to gather pastry into a ball of firm dough. Roll out two thirds of the pastry and line a 7 inch (18cm) flan dish. Reserve remainder for the top crust.

In a medium pan heat the oil. Add chopped onions and sauté until soft, add sliced mushrooms and cook a little more. Remove from the heat and stir in the miso paste, a little black pepper and possibly salt depending on the strength of the miso. Spread mixture in prepared pastry case, cover with sliced tomatoes followed by grated cheese. Roll out remaining pastry, paint rim of pastry in flan dish, cover pie with pastry. Trim edges with knife. Brush with a little milk or beaten egg if you wish, make a hole in the centre to let out the steam. Bake at 170°c for approx 40 minutes.

Serve with broccoli and carrots.

Onion Tart

pastry
6 oz (150g) plain flour
3 oz (75g) butter
2 oz (50g) mature cheddar cheese, grated
little water to mix

filling
little olive oil
2 lbs (1kg) onions, finely sliced
1 clove garlic, crushed
pinch freshly grated nutmeg
2 oz (50g) mature cheddar cheese, grated
salt and pepper
4 eggs, size 3
5 fl oz (125ml) double cream

In a large bowl, place flour, butter and salt and rub together until mixture resembles fine breadcrumbs. Stir in grated cheese and using your hands mix together with a little water gathering the pastry into a ball. Wrap in cling film and refrigerate for 20 minutes, then roll out to line an 8 inch (20cm) oiled flan dish. Prick all over with a fork and refrigerate for 30 minutes. Bake in a preheated oven for approx 15 minutes at 190°c.

Heat the olive oil in a large frying pan, add the onions and garlic and fry for approx 30 minutes until golden brown. Season with nutmeg, salt and pepper. Place in pre-baked pastry shell. Place eggs in a bowl and beat, add the cream and cheese and pour over the onions. Bake at 180°c for approx 20 minutes until set but still moist.

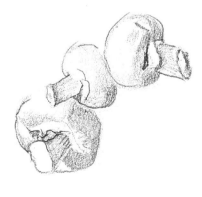

Spinach Pie

> 1 lb (450g) spinach, lightly steamed, chopped and well drained
> 6 spring onions, very finely chopped
> 12 oz (350g) cottage cheese, drained
> nutmeg, salt and black pepper
> 2 large eggs, beaten
> 1 lb (450g) ready made puff pastry

In a large bowl, mix together the spinach, spring onions and cottage cheese. Season with nutmeg, salt and pepper. Stir in beaten eggs, reserving a little to glaze the finished pie.

Take a spring clip cake tin approx 8 inches (20cm) in diameter $2^{1/4}$ inches (6cm deep). Oil the inside of the tin.

Take two thirds of the pastry and roll it out to line the tin. Fill it with the spinach mixture, then roll out the remaining pastry to cover the pie. Dampen edges to seal and crimp edges together. Paint the top of the pie with reserved egg and make a hole in the centre to let steam escape.

Bake at 190°c for approx 45 minutes until risen and golden.

Remove from the oven and leave to stand for 5 minutes, then release spring and with the help of two spatulas ease the pie off the bottom tin and onto a serving plate.

Serve hot with parsley carrots, or leave to cool and serve with salad.

Creative cookery lesson!

Vegetable Cobbler

Approx 2lbs (1 kg) mixed vegetables in season, cut into bite size pieces and steam until tender. Vegetables of varying density may need to be cooked separately or some will inevitably overcook.

sauce for vegetables
a little vegetable oil
1 large onion, finely chopped
1 clove garlic, crushed
1 can chopped tomatoes approx 14 oz (400g)
1 vegetable stock cube
1 bay leaf
1 teaspoon dried thyme
little water
salt and pepper
possibly a little cornflour

Cobbler
8 oz (225g) self raising flour, white or whole-wheat or a mix of both
1 teaspoon baking powder
2 oz (50g) butter
2 oz (50g) cheddar cheese, grated
1 egg, beaten and a little milk
1 tablespoon chopped parsley
pinch salt and cayenne pepper
little parmesan cheese for finishing

Place the cooked vegetables into a shallow baking dish.

In a small pan make the gravy or sauce. Sauté the onion and garlic in oil until soft and golden. Add bay leaf, thyme, tomatoes, water, stock cube and simmer to make a tasty pouring sauce. Season to taste with salt and pepper. If the mixture appears too watery, use a little cornflour to thicken. Pour over vegetables in baking dish.

Place flour, baking powder, salt, cayenne and butter into a large mixing bowl and rub together. Add grated cheese and parsley, mix together with the egg and sufficient milk to make a soft dough. Turn out onto a floured board, roll out to $1/2$ inch (1 cm) thickness and cut into small circles, approx 2 inches (5cm) in diameter and arrange on top of the vegetable mixture. Brush with a little milk, sprinkle with parmesan and bake at 180°c until risen and golden. Should only take about 20 minutes or even less, it depends on how warm the cooked vegetables and sauce are when cobbler is added, and then place in the oven.

Winter Vegetable Pie

pastry
8 oz (225g) plain flour, white or whole-wheat or a mix of both
5 oz (150g) butter, cut into small pieces
pinch salt and cayenne pepper
water to mix

filling
1 leek
1 small parsnip
2 carrots
$1/2$ pt (275ml) milk
1 oz (25g) butter
1 oz (25g) plain white flour
4 oz (110g) strong cheddar cheese
salt, pepper and nutmeg
little milk or beaten eggs to glaze

Place flour, butter, salt and pepper in a mixing bowl and rub together until the mixture resembles fine bread crumbs. Mix with a little water to gather pastry into a ball of firm dough. Take two thirds of the pastry and roll out to line a pie dish 8 inches (20cm) in diameter. Reserve the remainder for the top of the pie.

Cut the vegetables into bite size pieces and steam until tender, drain well.

In a medium saucepan melt the butter, mix in the flour and add the milk, stirring or whisking until a thick smooth sauce. Remove from heat, stir in grated cheese and season with salt, pepper and nutmeg.

Add the drained vegetables and stir, then place the mixture in the pastry case. Moisten edges with water. Roll out remaining pastry and cover the pie, taking care to seal the edges. Make a hole in the top for the steam to escape. Brush with a little milk or beaten egg if desired. Bake at 160°c for approx 40 minutes until golden.

SUE'S IDEAS ON SALADS & DRESSINGS

General Salad Information

Mayonnaise

Sweet Yellow Mayonnaise

Vinaigrette

Sesame Soy Dressing

Our salads are made freshly every day. Using a wide variety of vegetables, whenever possible we use organic produce. In the summer months in particular the garden is full of delicious vegetables, green salad and fruit, providing us with the best possible ingredients.

It is difficult to give exact recipes for salads. Almost any vegetables can be mixed together to achieve delicious and nutritious results. The most important factor is the freshness of the food being prepared. Therefore, the following salads are not precise recipes but suggestions leaving you to be creative and please your own palate.

A GREEN SALAD is an important part of most meals. Freshness of leaves is paramount; a variety of colour and shape pleases the eye as well as the taste buds. A favourite mix at the Centre would be, Lollo Rosso, Little Gem, Curly Endive with a little Rocket or perhaps lambs lettuce or Watercress to add a little spice.

AVOCADO sliced at the last moment before serving, dressed with a vinaigrette, or perhaps mixed with chopped chicory, parsley and a garlic vinaigrette. Avocados are also delicious mixed carefully into a tomato salad.

BEETROOT is usually served without a dressing. Often served raw, grated with a sweet apple also grated and mixed together. Or boiled and sliced or cubed.

CARROTS simply grated or cut into sticks and perhaps a little orange juice to keep them moist.

At the School and the Centre **ALFAFA** sprouts are served at each meal. We grow them in large jars on the windowsill, in about 5 days they are ready to eat. The sprouts are served unadorned.

COLESLAW is always popular. The usual mix is approximately one part grated carrot to three parts very finely shredded cabbage with a light sprinkling of currants and shredded gherkin, dressed with home made mayonnaise. You will find our recipe for mayonnaise at the end of this section.

CELERY is washed and dried, if necessary some of the strings removed (drying is important to prevent dressing from becoming watery) then finely chopped and mixed with chopped apple, dates or currants, a few chopped walnuts and dressed with sweet yellow mayonnaise. You will find the recipe for sweet yellow mayonnaise at the end of this section.

Prepared **CELERY** chopped and combined with a few green grapes and sliced green apples (skins left on) lightly dressed with lemon juice, perhaps the addition of diced cheddar cheese or some pumpkin seeds.

CELARIAC makes a delicious salad. Cut into fine sticks, dropped into a pot of boiling water to which lemon juice has been added for a moment or two. It should be well drained and cooled before dressing with parsley and a vinaigrette or mayonnaise.

COURGETTE cut into very fine sticks and dressed with a little olive oil, white wine vinegar, salt, pepper and dill. Sweetcorn kernels could be added for a change.

CUCUMBER sliced very thinly, dressed with olive oil, lemon salt and pepper, plenty of dill. Leave to marinate for an hour or so and drain before serving.

CUCUMBER grated, placed in a towel and all of the juice squeezed out. Then mixed with Greek yoghurt, salt and crushed garlic.

POTATOES should be boiled or steamed, peeled and left to cool. Then cut or sliced and mixed with chopped chives or finely sliced spring onions. Or perhaps cooked with fresh green peas and chopped mint. Dressed with a little mayonnaise. Another suggestion would be the addition of finely sliced red onion, a few capers or black olives dressed with sunflower oil, lemon juice, herb salt and pepper.
To give an Indian flavour, sauté sliced onion in a little oil, when softened add a little turmeric powder and curry powder, season well with salt, leave to cool, then mix with prepared potato, the addition of a few peas will make it very colourful. The combinations of potato salad are endless.

TOMATOES cut in any way you wish, skin and seeds left intact, or not, just as you wish. Dressed with olive oil, balsamic vinegar, basil salt and pepper. You could add black olives, a little red onion very finely sliced, perhaps some red green or yellow peppers finely sliced, or chives or parsley. When chopped cucumber is also added with fetta cheese you have a delicious Greek Salad.

PASTA should be cooked in the usual way and cooled, a little bouillon powder in the cooking water helps the final flavour of the salad. One way is to simply dress the pasta with pesto and season. Alternatively mixed with finely cut colourful peppers and black olives and dressed with a little vinegar and olive oil and seasoned well with herb salt, pepper, basil or oregano. Finally garnish with fresh parsley.

COUSCOUS (you will find the way to prepare couscous in the hot food section under Spicy Vegetables with Chickpeas and Couscous.) The couscous should be cooled and mixed with a few currants, plenty of finely chopped parsley, a few drops of lemon juice and seasoned with herb salt. Sweetcorn kernels could be added for a change or very finely chopped young courgette, perhaps some sesame seeds. Another addition could be finely chopped spring onions or chives.

RICE brown or white basmati works well. The rice should be cooked and quickly cooled and once the rice salad is made it should be placed in the refrigerator until served. Rice mixes well with finely chopped peppers or sweetcorn kernels, plenty of parsley, season well with a little lemon juice.
Indian style rice is always popular. Heat a little sunflower oil in a pan, when the oil is very hot throw in a few black mustard seeds, these should pop and jump, followed immediately by some chopped onion, reduce the heat and cook until the onions have softened then adding a little turmeric powder. Remove from the heat and set aside until cold. When it is quite cold stir into cooked rice, adding salt and lemon juice to taste. A few toasted cashew nuts can be added, or some cooked cooled garden peas, finally finish with a little chopped fresh coriander.

Mayonnaise

1 egg
1¹/2 tablespoons coarse grain made mustard
3 fl oz (75ml) white wine vinegar
salt and pepper to taste
15fl oz (500ml) sunflower oil

Place egg, mustard and vinegar into a food processor or liquidiser and blend, then slowly pour in the oil in a steady stream. Season and taste.

Sweet Yellow Mayonnaise

1 egg
1 tablespoon coarse grain made mustard
3 fl oz (75ml) white wine vinegar
2 oz (50g) chopped dates previously soaked
in a little hot water to soften them
¹/2 teaspoon of turmeric powder
a little salt
15fl oz (500ml) sunflower oil

Place egg, mustard, vinegar, turmeric powder and dates into a food processor liquidiser and blend. Pour in the oil in a steady stream. Add salt to taste.

Vinaigrette

1 level teaspoon salt
¹/2 clove garlic, well crushed
1 level teaspoon dry mustard powder
1 tablespoon white wine vinegar or balsamic vinegar
pepper
6 tablespoons oil, sunflower or olive oil

The above ingredients can be changed to suite individual tastes. Lemon juice can be used in place of vinegar. The garlic is optional, and chopped herbs can be added.

Place all the ingredients in a screw top jar and shake well.

Sesame Soy Dressing

1 tablespoon soy sauce
1 tablespoon tahini
1 tablespoon red wine vinegar
2 tablespoons sunflower oil
1 clove garlic, crushed
1 teaspoon fresh root ginger, grated
1 tablespoon toasted ground sesame seeds
3 tablespoons water (possibly a little more depending on consistency required)
little salt to taste

Blend all the ingredients together. This is a very strongly flavoured dressing.

SUE'S CAKES,
COOKIES & DESSERTS

Almond Tart

Apple and Almond Cake

Banana Raisin Teabread

Blackcurrant Cream

Brockwood Cookies

Carrot Cake

Chocolate Cake

Date and Orange Cake

Esme's Recipe for Wholemeal Scones

Greek Lemon Cake

Not So Naughty Cheesecake

Pineapple Meringue

Toffee Date Cake

Almond Tart

pastry
3 oz (75g) butter
2 oz (50g) caster sugar
5 oz (150g) plain flour
a little water
raspberry or apricot jam

filling
4 oz (110g) butter
4 oz (110g) caster sugar
2 oz (50g) self raising flour
2 oz (50g) ground almonds
2 eggs, beaten
few drops almond essence
few flaked almonds to finish

To make the pastry: place butter, sugar and flour in a mixing bowl and rub together until mixture resembles fine breadcrumbs. Gather with a little water to make a ball of firm dough. Turn on to a floured board and roll out to line a greased 8 inch (20cm) flan dish. Spread base with jam.

In a mixing bowl, cream together the butter and sugar, add the beaten eggs gradually with almond essence and beat well. Then fold in the flour and ground almonds. Spread the mixture carefully on top of the jam in pastry case, sprinkle with flaked almonds and bake for 40 - 50 minutes at 160°c until golden and firm.

Very good served warm with cream or custard as a pudding or cold as a teatime cake.

Apple and Almond Cake

5 oz (150g) butter
2 large eggs, beaten
8 oz (225g) caster sugar
1 teaspoon almond essence
6 oz (150g) self raising flour
2 oz (50g) ground almonds
$1^1/2$ teaspoons baking powder
12 oz (350g) cooking apples, peeled, cored and sliced
1 oz (25g) flaked almonds

Place the butter and sugar into a large mixing bowl and beat together until smooth and creamy. Beat in eggs and almond essence, add flour, ground almonds and baking powder and fold together; this will result in a stiff mixture.

Spread half the mixture in the base of an oiled lined 8 inch (20cm) loose bottomed cake tin. Cover with sliced apples. Place the remaining mixture on top in blobs and spread evenly. Sprinkle with flaked almonds and bake at 160°c for approx $1^1/2$ hours until evenly golden and cooked through.

Turn out and cool on a wire rack. Alternatively serve warm with whipped cream.

Banana Raisin Teabread

4 oz (110g) butter
3 ripe bananas
2 large eggs
5 oz (150g) soft brown sugar
9 oz (250g) whole-wheat flour
1 teaspoon cinnamon
2 rounded teaspoons baking powder
6 oz (175g) raisins
a little demerara sugar

Melt butter, add mashed bananas and eggs and beat well.

Place all dried ingredients into a large mixing bowl, pour in the butter, banana, egg mix and beat well.

Pour into an oiled and lined loaf tin, $4^1/2$ inches x 9 inches (12cm x 23cm). Sprinkle a little demerara sugar on the top and bake at 160°c for approx 1 hour.

Loaf is best when stored for at least one day before eating. Serve sliced with butter.

Blackcurrant Cream

Serves 6

1 lb (450g) blackcurrants, fresh or frozen
little water
$^1/2$ pt (275ml) milk + 2 tablespoons
$^1/2$ oz (10g) cornflour
2 oz (50g) caster sugar
$^1/2$ pt (275ml) double cream
caster sugar to taste

Place the blackcurrants (with just sufficient water to stop them from burning) in a small saucepan. Bring to simmer and cook until fruit is soft. Then push the contents of the saucepan through a sieve discarding any skins etc that will not go through. Set aside.

Place the cornflour, sugar and 2 tablespoons of milk in a small basin and mix to a paste. Heat the $^1/2$ pt (275ml) milk in a small saucepan and bring to the boil. Pour onto the cornflour paste, mix, then turn it back into the saucepan. Return to the boil stirring all the time. Cook for a moment or two then set aside to cool.

Place cream into a large bowl and whisk until thick. Fold in blackcurrant liquid and cooled cornflour. Taste and add more sugar if necessary. Spoon into 6 ramekin dishes or into a serving bowl. Place in refrigerator to cool.

Before serving decorate with extra cream and fruit if desired.

Brockwood Cookies

4 oz (110g) butter
4 oz (110g) plain whole-wheat flour
4 oz (110g) rolled oats
2 oz (50g) desiccated coconut
2 oz (50g) currants
few drops vanilla essence
a little milk

Into a large mixing bowl place flour and butter and rub together until mixture resembles fine breadcrumbs. Mix in oats, sugar, coconut and currants. Add vanilla and sufficient milk to gather mixture together into a ball. Turn onto a floured surface, roll out to approx $^1/4$ inch (5mm) thickness and cut into shapes. Place on an oiled baking tray and prick all over with a fork. Bake for 15 to 20 minutes at 170°c.

When cool, remove from tray and serve or store in an airtight tin.

Carrot Cake

4 oz (110g) walnuts, chopped
8 oz (225g) carrots, peeled and finely grated
5 oz (150g) whole-wheat self raising flour
8 oz (225g) soft light brown sugar
1 teaspoon bicarbonate of soda
1 teaspoon ground cinnamon
8 oz (225g) butter, melted
3 eggs, beaten
1 teaspoon vanilla essence

frosting
8 oz (225g) full fat cream cheese (low fat will not work)
2 oz (50g) unsalted butter
2 oz (50g) icing sugar
zest and juice of 1 orange
few chopped walnuts to finish

In a large mixing bowl mix together nuts, carrots, flour, sugar, cinnamon and bicarbonate of soda.

In a separate container blend together melted butter, eggs and vanilla essence. Pour in to dry ingredients and mix well. Spoon into an 8 inch (20cm) deep round cake tin, which has been oiled and lined with greaseproof paper. Bake at 170°c for approx 1 hour. Test with a fine skewer to see if baked through.

When cake is quite cold, slice across the middle making two rounds.

To make the frosting, beat together the cream cheese, butter, sugar and orange zest in a large bowl, adding a little orange juice to give a thick creamy texture. Sandwich together the two halves of the cake with about 1/3 of the frosting. Spread the remainder on the top and the side of the cake, finish with chopped nuts.

The finished cake will store in the refrigerator for up to 1 week. The cake without the frosting will freeze well.

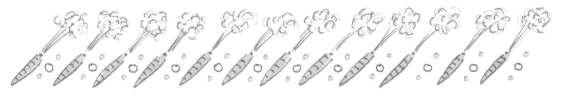

Chocolate Cake

$^1/_4$ pt (150ml) sunflower oil

$^1/_4$ pt (150ml) yoghurt

5 tablespoons (75ml) golden syrup or clear honey

6 oz (175g) soft light brown sugar

8 oz (225g) white self raising flour

2 tablespoons cocoa

$^1/_2$ teaspoon bicarbonate of soda

pinch of salt

3 large eggs

topping

3 tablespoons apricot jam

5 oz (150g) dark chocolate

$^1/_4$ pt (150ml) double cream

In a large mixing bowl beat together the oil, yoghurt, syrup/honey and eggs. Add sugar, beat, sift in remaining dry ingredients and beat well. Pour mixture into an oiled, lined 8 inch round deep cake tin. Bake for approx 1$^1/2$ hours at 160°c.

In a small saucepan, gently melt together chocolate broken into small pieces and double cream, allow to stand until spreadable consistency. Placing in the refrigerator can speed up this process, but take care as mixture could become too hard.

When cake is cool, spread with apricot jam and cover with the chocolate cream mix.

This cake is moist and will keep or freeze well.

Wholemeal scones and cream

Esme's Recipe for Wholemeal Scones

1$\frac{1}{4}$ lbs (650g/4 cups) 100% organic stone-ground wholemeal flour
4 tablespoons soft brown sugar
2 heaped teaspoons baking powder
6 oz (175g) vegetable margarine or butter cut into small pieces
6 oz (175g) chopped dates
1 large egg, beaten
approx $\frac{1}{2}$ pt (275ml) milk (quantity varies depending on texture of flour)

Place flour, sugar, baking powder and margarine or butter in a large mixing bowl and rub together until mixture resembles fine breadcrumbs. Add the chopped dates and mix. Stir in beaten egg with sufficient milk to make mixture into a firm dough.

Turn onto a floured surface and roll out till approx 3/4 inch (2mm thick). Cut into rounds using a 2$\frac{1}{2}$ inch cutter. Place on an oiled baking tray. Should make about 24 scones.

Bake in a hot oven 200°c for 13 - 15 minutes until cooked through, remove from oven and cool on wire rack.

Scones should be stored in the fridge in a covered container. When needed they can be heated through in the oven or heated under the grill. Serve warm with butter.

Greek Lemon Cake

6 oz (175g) white self raising flour
1 teaspoon baking powder
4 oz (110g) butter
5 oz (150g) caster sugar
2 large eggs
grated zest of 1 large lemon
little milk

topping
2 oz (50g) icing sugar
juice of 1 large lemon

Cream together butter and sugar, add beaten eggs, beat well, fold in flour with baking powder and grated lemon zest, add a little milk to make a soft dropping consistency. Take care not to make the mixture too wet or the cake will sink. Turn mixture into an oiled, lined 6 inch (15cm) deep cake tin and bake for approx 45 minutes 160°c.

In a small saucepan heat juice and icing sugar together and pour over hot cake. Leave to cool for a while before removing from the tin.

Not So Naughty Cheesecake

crust

6 oz (150g) whole-wheat flour

1 level teaspoon baking powder

3 oz (75g) butter or margarine

2 oz (50g) caster sugar

filling

12 oz (350g) cottage cheese

2 eggs

$1/4$ pt (150ml) yoghurt

1 teaspoon vanilla essence

zest and juice of $1/2$ lemon

3 oz (75g) caster sugar

Crust: Place all the ingredients together into a mixing bowl and rub together until mixture resembles fine breadcrumbs. It will not roll, so thumb it into an 8 inch (20cm) oiled flan dish and bake at 160°c for 15 minutes.

Meanwhile prepare the filling. Place all the ingredients into a blender and blend until mixture is smooth. Pour into the pre-baked flan and bake for 30 - 40 minutes at 150°c until set.

Serve cold topped with fruit of your choice.

Date and Orange Cake

1 generous tablespoon golden syrup or honey

2 oz (50g) soft brown sugar

zest and juice of 1 large orange

$1/4$ pt (150ml) vegetable oil

2 fl oz (55ml) water

2 large eggs

9 oz (250g) whole-wheat flour

2 heaped teaspoons baking powder

7 oz (200g) chopped dates

In a large mixing bowl, mix together golden syrup/honey, sugar, water, oil, juice and zest of orange. Add eggs and beat well. Fold in flour, baking powder and chopped dates and mix well.

Pour into an oiled and lined round cake tin 7 inches (18cm) in diameter. Bake for approx $1 1/2$ hours at 150°c until golden and cooked through.

Pineapple Meringue

2 oz (50g) butter
2 oz (50g) plain white flour
1 oz (25g) caster sugar
$^1/_2$ pt (275ml) milk
$^1/_4$ pt (150ml) pineapple juice
12 oz (350g) pineapple, cut into small pieces (canned works well but fresh is better)
2 egg yolks

meringue
2 egg whites
4 oz (100g) caster sugar

Melt the butter in a medium saucepan, stir in the flour and sugar, slowly add the juice and milk stirring all the time until sauce thickens. Cook for a minute or two, continue stirring. Remove from the heat, beat in the egg yolks, stir in the pineapple pieces. Spoon mixture into 6 buttered ramekin dishes.

Place the egg whites in a large clean bowl and whisk until very stiff, should be able to turn bowl upside down without egg falling out, however do not overwhisk. Add sugar a little at a time whisking until all is incorporated. Now meringue can be spooned on the top of the dishes or piped, whichever is best for you.

Place ramekins on a baking sheet. Bake at 140°c for 30 minutes. Serve hot or cold.

Toffee Date Cake

2 oz (50g) softened butter
6 oz (175g) dark brown soft sugar
8 oz (225g) white self raising flour
6 oz (175g) dates, stoned and chopped
1 large egg, whisked
1 teaspoon vanilla essence
1 teaspoon bicarbonate of soda
1/2 pt (275ml) boiling water

In a large mixing bowl, cream together butter and sugar and beat in whisked egg. In a separate container, place dates, bicarbonate of soda and vanilla, pour on boiling water and mix, the mixture will foam. Add this alternately with the flour to the creamed mixture, beat well. Pour mixture into an oiled and lined 7 inch (18cm) round deep cake tin. Bake for approx 45 minutes at 160°c.

topping
2 1/2 oz (60g) dark brown soft sugar
1 1/2 oz (40g) unsalted butter
2 tablespoons double cream

Place all the ingredients into a small saucepan, melt together, bring to the boil and simmer for 3 minutes. Leave to cook, this will take some time.

Spread over the cold cake. Alternatively serve the cake hot as a pudding pouring over the hot sauce before serving.

Inwoods, the small school at Brockwood.

The Brockwood vegetable garden.

Raman Patel - An Introduction

Before coming to Brockwood in 1980 I had very little experience in cooking. I was accepted as a staff member on the condition that I was to work in the garden though when I arrived I was informed that the kitchen had only women staff and they desperately needed a man to help lift heavy loads. I thought this might at last be my chance to develop my biceps so I took up the challenge. Within a few months of my working, Geraldine who used to be in charge of the kitchen left and the baton in the form of a hot potato was passed on to me. I felt I was thrown in at the deep end and before I knew it I was cooking for a hundred plus people. Little did I know that within the next three months that number would increase tenfold as it was the time for the annual gatherings.

In the kitchen, cooking turned out to be only one aspect of the work. There was the ordering and the finding of good quality food, keeping the larders stocked, maintaining good relationships with the suppliers and working within the allocated budget. Then there was the question of what kind of food to cook, regarding which there are hundreds of approaches, philosophies and schools of thought, each claiming theirs to be the best. Knowing this, we did not ascribe to any one of them in particular. Food and health being an important part of life, due consideration was given to it while seeing how this might fit in the larger picture of what constitutes good health. When one loses a larger perspective, it is easy to become obsessed and neurotic about food and health. It can become a religion of sorts, believing it to be the cure for all the ills of man. We had to be careful that we did not, for reasons of our own, prescribe or impose a particular diet on others. Not that there was no room for personal experimentation with food either due to ill health or otherwise. In fact some did go on fruit, juice or raw food diets and the kitchen catered for those who had certain peculiarities or allergies regarding the intake of food. As a matter of fact, some of the students when they first arrived were not necessarily vegetarians. Many were quite young and had left their homes for the first time and often felt homesick. With the towns being far away and with very little entertainment available in the countryside, food became one of the central focal points. Coupled with all this, if the food was not flavoursome, the students longed for home and the food that they were familiar with. We had to come up with food that was palatable and at the same time nutritious. It also had to be varied since in any given year more than twenty-five countries were represented.

Though limited in supply, the garden produced excellent organically grown vegetables, herbs and fruits. Organically grown meant that along with the produce came a fair share of bugs, slugs, caterpillars, snails and even spiders to name but a few. Being vegetarians we could not afford to see any of them ending up on somebody's plate! Anyone who had a romantic philosophy regarding organic versus non-organic food was tested to the limit when thirty pounds of freezing spinach had to be carefully washed, especially in the late autumn with freezing water. Then there were fifty pounds of potatoes and parsnips that had to be gone over thoroughly like a sculptor with his tool. Since organic produce does not necessarily follow the laws of uniformity, buried deep in all sorts of crevices, corners and nooks were all those little creatures that had made their homes and food larders and had to be coaxed into giving them up. The garden staff under Gary and Antonio's eye kept pushing, firmly but gently, boxes upon boxes of such produce. In the end though it was worth all the trouble since compared to the non-organic food, the flavour and the nutritional quality of the organic produce was unmatchable.

The most demanding and challenging aspect while working in the kitchen was that of relationships. While this applied to all the areas of the school, in the kitchen the added factors were that we had to work together as a team in a small area with time constraints. Every day three meals had to be prepared, and on time. Failing to do so affected the schedule of the rest of the school. Since questioning everything has always been the spirit of the school, there was no reason why that spirit would not *spill* over in the kitchen. Questions regarding authority, freedom, control and trust would often come up. To address these issues took time and energy, especially when a new person joined the team. In our society, everything is kept under control and check by use of authority, power and fear, thereby freedom or apparent freedom is denied. When the lid of authority is lifted, the best and worst aspects of a person can come out. But in the absence of any authority, just to have freedom without the presence of intelligence, an important *ingredient*, is definitely a *recipe* for disaster if not anarchy. All these questions had to be gone into and for me there was much learning. At a personal level, before I came to Brockwood, I was often offered a position of responsibility in the various jobs that I did. I always declined, because it meant taking responsibility for so-called irresponsible people. The reason why I took the responsibility at Brockwood when offered was because here everyone was at least interested to learn about the nature of self. So if and when difficulties and problems arose, and they did, mini Mahabharatas of sorts you may say, there was the intention to resolve them. The time I was in the kitchen, I was interested to see how I can work and at the same time make myself dispensable. I can go on and on but for now I will leave it on the back burner.

If I were to narrate the countless heartrending, comical, frustrating, affectionate and confusing interactions that transpired between people, it would take pages and I would only repeat what Sue Gerard has captured extremely well in her introduction. I must though narrate one such interaction since it has to do with food. Because of the international nature of the school, the usage of the language (which came to be known as "Brock Speak") often created mind-boggling misunderstandings, frustrations and above all much laughter. Dorothy Simmons who was then the principal of the school, and had been assigned to make toast for everyone at breakfast, noticed a student not having any toast so she inquired if he wanted some. "No, I am fed up", he said. Dorothy looked rather concerned and asked what was the matter. "Nothing is the matter, I am just fed up, I have already eaten too much", came the reply! Did you know that the other name for museli is "mouse lee"?

In the kitchen we had many in-jokes and knowing each other's tendencies we had much fun pulling each other's legs. When I heard words like "Come on then" from Sue or "What time is it?" from Pippa, I knew it was time for me to brew a pot of ginger tea (chai). When there was any delay on my part to move on with the assigned task, it was the unmistakably voice of Francies that you heard, "Are we not having chai today?" The message was loud and clear. There was no time to waste!

During the fifteen years I worked in the kitchen, I did manage to go out in the garden, teach basic electronics and at times English as a Foreign Language (EFL). But my main work remained in the kitchen, both at the school and the centre. Since I am now doing some of the other Krishnamurti-related work, when I come and work at Brockwood, it feels as though I have just returned home from being away.

Raman Patel

COMPLEMENTARY DISHES

· · · · · · · · · · · · · ·

Chapati

Deep Fried Pooris

Cucumber Raita

PÂTÉ

· · · · · · · · · ·

Tofu Pâté

Smoke Flavoured Aubergine Pâté

Olive/Capers/Sundried Tomatoes Pâté

Avocado Pâté (Guacamole)

SAUCES

· · · · · · · · · · · · · ·

All Purpose Pomarola Tomato Sauce

Versions 1 & 2

Pesto Sauce

Mushroom Sauce

All Purpose Curry Sauce

Chapati

Chapatis, often called rotis are cooked all over India. They are unleavened bread made from a wheat flour and are very quick and simple to make. Traditionally they are baked on clay Tava (plate). Instead, you can use an iron griddle or a non-stick skillet. With a little practice and patience, you can master the art of turning out perfectly round, thin, puffy and melt-in-the mouth chapatis. Of the many items to come out of an Indian kitchen for any given meal, chapatis are always the last as they are best when eaten hot. It is amazing to see mothers turn them out one after another, keeping a watchful eye on everything and knowing whose turn it is next while you impatiently await yours. Here all hierarchies, favouritism and "me first" have no place! If the chapatis are prepared ahead of time, it is mind-boggling to see (especially in those extended families) a huge pile extending over 12 inches (30cms) in no time at all, reduced to an empty space! It does make you wonder how day after day, year after year, next to a hot stove, and with hardly a single complaint is this feat possible? Not only that, but mothers are always the last ones to eat. Is it love or lack of emancipation?

8 oz (225g) finely milled and sifted whole wheat flour
1¹/2 tablespoons cooking oil
³/4 teaspoon salt
7 fl oz (210ml) boiling water

In a large bowl place flour, salt and oil. Rub until a somewhat crumbly texture develops. Pour boiling water over it and mix with a spoon. When the mixture feels a little cooler, use your hand to collect the whole mass in a ball and turn it onto a work surface. Knead it for about 5 minutes to make it into a smooth and pliable dough. The amount of water absorbed will depend on the dryness of the flour. Cover with a damp cloth and set aside for half an hour. Divide the dough into 10 small balls and roll out on lightly floured surface into thin rounds approx 6-7 inches (15-17 cms). Bake on a hot griddle or a nonstick skillet, placing the topside first. When little bubbles appear, turn over and cook for about a minute and turn over again. Press gently on all the sides with a cloth and if the skillet has the right amount of heat, and the consistency of the dough is correct, (not too dry) the chapati will puff up into a perfect ball. Apply a little butter or ghee (clarified butter) to the cooked chapatis and stack them together. This will keep them soft and warm. If you do not want to apply any fat, stack them in a container with a lid. Eat them with any curried dishes or pâtés.

Deep Fried Pooris

To include pooris in your repertoire of cooking once in a while makes for an interesting change. Unlike chapatis that do not use any fat while cooking, nor retain their fluffiness, pooris are deep fried and they come out like little crisp balloons and retain their shape unless the air is compressed out.

As children we would long for the day when pooris were on the menu. On such days, while playing cricket in the courtyard, the enticing faint whiff from the kitchen would drift by and suddenly as a result of anticipatory feast, all interest in the game would totally vanish. Especially on such days, for no apparent reason or logic, from no where as it were, friends and relatives would suddenly descend upon the house, and as is the custom in any Indian home to always offer food to the visitors, explained for the sudden disappearance of those heaps of pooris. Poor mothers!

4 oz (110g) finely milled whole meal flour
4 oz (110g) plain flour
3/4 teaspoon of salt
4fl oz (110ml) boiling water (may vary a little)
2 tablespoons vegetable oil for the dough and extra for deep frying

for spiced pooris
1/2 teaspoon turmeric
1 teaspoon cumin powder
1/2 teaspoon coriander
1/4 teaspoon chili

In a large bowl, mix the flours with salt. Add and rub in oil until a crumbly texture develops. Slowly and in stages, add water and mix with a spoon until the mixture feels a little cooler. Use your hand to collect the mass into a ball and turn it onto a work surface and knead it for about 10 minutes into a smooth and firm dough. Apply a little oil and keep it covered in a bowl for half an hour. Knead the dough again to incorporate any dryness formed on the outside. Divide into 18 balls and roll each out into about 4 inch (10 cm) circles covering each with a cloth or a cling film. If you do not have a karhai (an Indian style wok), fill up a deep fryer or a small deep pan with 2 inch (5cm) of oil, heat it until very hot. Very carefully place one poori on top of the oil. It will sink and as quickly begin to surface. With a draining spoon gently keep pushing and releasing the poori into the oil at different points and the poori will puff up in a few seconds. Turn the poori over and cook for about 10 - 15 seconds and remove it from the oil. Repeat and stack them up on a large plate. If you make the pooris for the first time for friends, wait for the often asked question "what is inside it?" Serve with spiced aubergine, any pâté or chick pea curry.

Cucumber Raita

There are many varieties of cucumbers the most common being the long, green variety usually grown under glass. This idea of growing under glass is not new. Even during the time of the Roman Emperor Tiberius, 'imperial' cucumbers were grown on beds with wheels and, as the weather turned cold, they were rolled under frames glazed with transparent stone!

The outside varieties of cucumber are shorter and are produced parthenogetically because if pollinated they develop an unpalatable, bitter taste. They can be windy and difficult to digest and many people experience irritable 'repeats'. Opinions have varied for a long time as to what part of the cucumber produces indigestion. The Japanese have now come up with cucumbers that are not bitter and are burp-free.

Traditionally, this relish is eaten with hot curries and also when the weather is hot.

24 fl oz (650 ml) plain thick yoghurt
4 oz (110 g) cucumber, peeled and grated
2 tablespoons finely chopped mint or dill
1/2 teaspoon cumin seeds
1/2 teaspoon coriander seeds
3/4 teaspoon salt

In a heavy-based frying pan, roast the seeds until they change colour and give off an aroma. Grind them in the coffee grinder. Place all the ingredients in a bowl and mix well. Chill before serving with any curry.

Gopal the kitchen magician.

Tofu Pâté

Tofu is a cheese from what are popularly and commonly known as Soya beans. They are a native to eastern Asia where the wild form still grows. The first record of its cultivation comes from China and dates back to 2838 BC. Soya beans have such versatile properties. They are best known as the source of an edible oil and the plant is now cultivated on a large scale in the U.S.A. In many parts of the world and particularly in the Far East they are eaten as a vegetable either unripe or ripe; the unripe seeds are eaten together with the pod. Sometimes the Soya beans are fermented and used for the preparation of Soya sauce or turned into a cake called Tempe. They are also eaten as sprouts and often dried and turned into flour. There is an increasing demand for Soya milk and their products, even ice creams.

Tofu until recently was only known for being used in Far Eastern restaurants. Now most health shops and large supermarkets have it on their shelves. Apart from being rich in protein, it contains calcium, vitamins and minerals. It is also low in calories and fat. No wonder that recently Soya beans are having a lot of press coverage regarding genetic tampering.

Tofu is available in health shops in an organic form and without any genetic modifications. People often say that tofu is rather flat and boring. With a little seasoning you can turn it into quite a delicious food. This recipe is simple and quick to make. The tofu pâté can be eaten spread on bread, toast, cracker and chips.

> 1 lb 2 oz (500g) firm tofu
> $2^{1}/_{2}$ tablespoons lemon juice
> $^{1}/_{2}$ teaspoon salt
> 3 tablespoons finely chopped fresh dill or 1 tablespoon dry
> 2 tablespoons lightly roasted ground sesame seeds

Remove the tofu from its wrapper and rinse under cold water. Remove excess water from it by pressing it in a cloth. Blend all the ingredients in the food processors and blend until smooth.

Picnic at Inwoods.

Smoke Flavoured Aubergine Pâté

3 tablespoons olive oil

1 medium red onion

3lbs 3oz (1.5kg) or 4 medium aubergines

$^1/_4$ teaspoon turmeric

$^1/_2$ tablespoon curry powder

2 cloves garlic, pressed

$^1/_2$ teaspoon salt

$^1/_4$ teaspoon cayenne pepper, optional

3 tablespoons freshly chopped coriander if available

Place the whole aubergines on a baking tray and grill for approx 20 minutes. Turn the aubergines a couple of times until the skins are charred and the flesh is cooked through. Remove the skins while they are still hot and chop them very small and put aside along with any juice that may come out while chopping. If you do not have a grill, roast the aubergines over the flame of the gas cooker, this method and with grilling gives them a distinct smoke flavour. Alternatively bake them in an oven at 180°c (350°f) for 30-50 minutes until soft to touch. Heat the oil in a non-stick frying pan and sauté the onions until transparent. Add garlic, all the spices, salt and coriander and cook for another minute. Add the aubergines and cook until all the water evaporates.

This recipe definitely has an exotic and a smoked flavour which awakes associations with the Mediterranean. Eat it spread on bread, toast, crackers or tortilla chips. It is also very good with pooris and chapatis (see recipes in this book) or simply serve cold as a salad.

Olive/Capers/Sundried Tomatoes Pâté *Serves 4 - 6*

The three ingredients, olives, capers and tomatoes grow well in the Mediterranean regions. When combined together as a pâté, it makes a rich spread with multi-purpose uses. Olive trees are botanically known as olea europeaea and are native to the eastern part of the Mediterranean region. They were cultivated by the ancient Egyptians, Greeks and the Romans. Now the largest producing countries are Spain, Italy and Greece. Olives are green when unripe and turn purplish when ripe and both are pickled and preserved in brine. The ripe olives are most prized for their oil. Cold pressed oil has high levels of mono unsaturated fats and is considered to bring down blood cholesterol levels. Studies have shown that in Greece and South Italy where it is consumed in large quantities, people have lower cholesterol levels.

All along the Mediterranean, caper plants can be seen growing wild, clinging to the walls. They are the unopened floral buds of the plant and have a strong pungent flavour, and when used with discretion, can enliven many dishes.

Sundried tomatoes have become fairly popular in recent years. When dried in the sun, the tomatoes seem to capture something inexplicable about the sky and the earth.

>8 oz (225g) sun dried tomato paste
>2 oz (50g) green olives, pitted
>2 oz (50g) black olives, pitted
>1 oz (25g) capers

Rinse and soak olives and capers in water for about four hours to remove the excess salt from them. Combine all the ingredients in a food processor and blend until a smooth paste results. Use sparingly on toast, bread, mix in bean salads or put a little in omelettes.

Avocado Pâté (Guacamole)

Avocados originally come from the mountainous regions of Mexico. Where else! They come in different varieties, shapes and sizes. The smallest one, often called baby avocado looks like a tiny courgette and is seedless. Amongst the middle size variety, the most familiar are the ones with smooth green skins. The less popular but the one with the best flavour is the Hass variety. They come in crinkly purplish skins. Then there is the giant variety, which is not very often seen and each avocado can yield up to 1 kg of pulp.

Avocados are prized for their nutty taste and high oil content (25 - 30 per cent) that is why in tropical countries they have been given the name "poor man's butter".

Guacamole is a dip made out of the avocados and very popular in Mexico. Many recipes include tomatoes, olives and bell peppers, which tend to discolour the pâté. The following recipe does not include any of those ingredients in order to leave the fresh look with its lovely green. Eat with bread, toast, crackers or with tortilla chips. Can also use as a dip for some raw vegetables.

- 1 tablespoon olive oil
- 1¹/2 tablespoons lemon juice
- 1 small onion finely chopped
- ¹/4 teaspoon salt
- ¹/2 green chilli, seeded and very finely chopped
- 3 large ripe avocados
- 2 tablespoons fresh coriander or oregano finely chopped

Peel and stone the avocados and place them in a bowl with lemon juice and salt. Mash them with a fork, add remaining ingredients and mix well.

Inwoods children looking for the wild guacamole

All Purpose Pomarola Tomato Sauce
Versions 1 & 2

The garden at Brockwood produces tons of tomatoes in the green house and most of them are used for the salads. In the late summer, when the tomatoes begin to fall to the ground, it is a good time to collect them to make into the sauce. The organically home grown tomatoes have an unbeatable flavour and aroma to them. A student once told me that if you have spent some time in the garden, it is very likely that at some time in your life you are bound to at least grow your own tomatoes if not have a small vegetable garden.

I have given two versions of the tomato sauce. The first is the most basic one and can generally be used for most pasta dishes that are baked in the oven. The second one is much richer with a fuller body as more vegetables are included in making the sauce. This sauce can be used with pasta dishes that are not baked, any grains, steamed vegetables, boiled or steamed potatoes, beans, peas or with lentils.

Version 1
Serves 4

6 tablespoons virgin olive oil
1 large onion finely chopped
3lbs 3oz (1.5kg) fresh ripe plum tomatoes blanched, skinned seeded and chopped or 2lbs 2oz (1kg) plum tomatoes with the juice
1 teaspoon salt
1/2 teaspoon sugar or 1 teaspoon honey
1/4 teaspoon freshly ground black pepper
1 tablespoon dry basil and a few leaves of fresh basil if available

Heat the oil in a medium and heavy saucepan and sauté the onions until transparent. Add the tinned tomatoes and the juice. If using ripe tomatoes, pour boiling water over them and allow them to sit for a while. Remove from water, peel skin and cut them into halves. Squeeze each half gently and shake your hand over the sink to allow the seeds to fall out through your fingers without losing the pulp. Cut them into small pieces and add to the onions along with salt and sugar or honey. Cook uncovered over medium heat stirring occasionally until the sauce thickens. Using the food processor or hand blender, blend the sauce until it is smooth. If the sauce is too thick add a little water. Rub dry basil between your palms and along with the black pepper, add it to the sauce. Before serving, garnish with roughly chopped basil. If you prefer, add a little olive oil at the end. The sauce will keep up to a week in the fridge and for months in the freezer.

Version 2

all the ingredients as version 1 plus:
1 medium carrot grated, finely chopped
2 sticks celery finely chopped
$1/2$ teaspoon oregano
$1/2$ teaspoon marjoram
large bunch parsley

Add carrot and celery after the onions are cooked and cook for five minutes further with the lid on. Follow the same procedure as in version 1 and add the oregano, marjoram and parsley along with the dry basil.

Pesto Sauce

Sweet basil, ocimum basilicum, is a perennial plant. It appears to be native to tropical Asia and Africa and was introduced into temperate regions where it is used in producing culinary delights. Basil comes in many varieties; the commonest one is with large and smooth green leaves. Both fresh and dry basil is used in cooking. For the purposes of making the pesto sauce, only the fresh and broad leaf variety is used. The plant will very easily grow in a pot if left by a sunny windowsill. Rinse them very lightly to remove the dust, as you do not want to wash away any of its flavour or scent. Incidentally, the specific epithet of basilicum appears to be derived from the Greek name for the King basiltis, or from its diminutive form basilus meaning a dragon-like creature with flaming breath! Perhaps a hint to those pesto makers and lovers of garlic?

Many species of pine trees yield edible seeds. They are known commercially as pignolias and the Italians call them pinocchio. Most edible seeds are found in North America and the seeds were mostly eaten by the natives who collected the entire strobili (cones) or obtained the seeds in huge quantity from the nests of pack rats, which store them for the winter! For our purposes, we need not go to such extremes as a stroll down to the supermarket and a little dig in the pocket would adequately accomplish the task.

> 6 - 8 tablespoons virgin olive oil
> 4 oz (110g) fresh basil leaves, stalks removed
> 3 oz (75g) pine nuts
> 3 - 4 cloves garlic
> 1/4 teaspoon salt
> 4 tablespoons grated parmesan cheese, optional - may be served separately

Food processor method

Blend in the food processor all the dry ingredients to a gritty paste. Keep the motor running and slowly add the oil through the opening of the lid. Remove and store it in a glass jar. In the fridge the pesto will last a week and for months in the freezer. Add enough oil in the jar so that it covers the pesto.

Mortar and pestle method

Adding a few leaves at a time, grind them into a paste. Remove and set aside. Place chopped garlic along with the pine nuts into the mortar and repeat the process until a smooth paste results. Mix in prepared basil and incorporate it well with garlic and pine nuts. Add in the parmesan now if included, stirring constantly add the oil.

Serve with pasta, steamed vegetables, beans or vegetable salads, baked or steamed potatoes or simply spread it on toast or crackers.

In this recipe, pine nuts are used and favoured over the other nuts, as they have a piny flavour to them and seem to combine well with basil. If you can't find pine nuts, other nuts may be used.

Mushroom Sauce

At and around Brockwood there are many woods and often the students and the visitors returning from a walk would pick and bring in the mushrooms they had come across. Some of them did not know if they were edible, while others would swear to their non-poisonous status. Well, when you are cooking for a large number of people and are not dead sure if they are edible, it is better to be safe than sorry. There is a story of a family returning from mushroom picking and the little boy who was naughty was refused dinner while the others feasted. Next day, he was the only one left from his family to walk the funeral march! Hope this is by no means a deterrent since not all the mushrooms are poisonous and a very few are actually deadly. To include some wild mushrooms along with the cultivated ones can really enhance the dish. Mushrooms grow amongst deciduous coniferous, birch and beech trees. The most common one is psalliota campestirs, commonly known as the white or the button mushroom. The most expensive, the best, and considered to be the most delicious all over Europe is boletus edulis. It is commonly known as cep in France, steinpilz in Germany and porcini in Italy.

Some of the other edible and popular mushrooms are parasol, chanterelle, the giant puffball, straw, oyster, morels and shikate. The best way to cook the mushrooms is over high heat. This way some of their juices get sealed in and what does get released evaporates while cooking.

4 tablespoons olive oil
1/2 oz (12g) dried wild boletus edulis mushrooms, soaked
1 1/2 lbs (700g) button mushrooms washed & sliced
1 pt (1/2 ltr) milk
2 oz (50g) butter
1 teaspoon thyme
1 1/2 teaspoons nutmeg, freshly grated
1/2 tablespoon plain flour
2 cloves garlic, pressed
1 oz (25g) chopped capers, optional
1 teaspoon salt
3 tablespoons finely chopped parsley

Soak the dried mushrooms in about 10 fl oz (300ml) of warm water for half an hour. Remove from the water and carefully rinse to remove any sediment and chop roughly. In a large frying pan over high heat sauté them with the fresh mushrooms until all the water has evaporated and the mushrooms have nicely browned. Set aside. In a medium size heavy bottom pan bring the milk to a boil. In another similar pan, melt the butter and fry the garlic for 30 seconds. Add the flour and with a wire whisk mix it well. Cook on very low heat for 2 - 3 minutes making sure it does not burn or form lumps. Add half of the boiling milk and quickly and vigorously whisk the mixture in order to avoid it forming any lumps. Add remaining milk, whisk and gently bring it almost to a boil and cook for about five minutes. Mix in the cooked mushrooms, add salt, capers, thyme and nutmeg and stir them in. Add parsley before serving. The sauce is best when served immediately otherwise coat the surface with melted butter to prevent a skin forming.

All Purpose Curry Sauce

Serves 6

Before the British rule in India, curry powder as a commercial mixture did not exist. Traditionally, each family in India had their special mixture of spices that was handed down from generation to generation. Many British people in India had taken a liking and had become addicted to Indian cuisine. So for export purposes, an easy to use curry powder was invented. It is made from a mixture of certain spices like coriander seeds, cumin seeds, fenugreek, black pepper, turmeric, dried ginger and dried chilli. It is believed that the name curry came from kaari leaves, murraya koenigii, a tree belonging to the same family as the neem. Thanks to the British curry powder is now a household name worldwide. The curious twist to this episode is that the curry powder is now prepared in England by Indians from Africa. It has become so popular that it is even exported to Madras! Isn't globalization meant to be a hot topic?

In Indian cooking the sauce is an important feature and is made by blending onions, fresh ginger, garlic and tomatoes to a smooth paste. Alternatively chop the ingredients very finely. The secret of a good sauce is to cook without burning it until it browns and develops a rich colour and an appetising aroma. This sauce can be used for any dish containing dried beans, lentils (dhals) peas and fresh vegetables. In order to make homemade ground spices, roast the seeds or whole spices in a heavy frying pan over a low heat until they just turn brown and give off their aroma. Powder them in a coffee blender and store them in airtight jars. If the recipe calls for garam masala (it produces body heat and is used at the end of the cooking process), roast and blend 2 oz (50 g) cinnamon sticks, 1 tablespoon cloves, 1 tablespoon black pepper and 2 tablespoons black or green cardamom pods. There are dishes that do not use a sauce at all but only spices and ingredients that a particular recipe may call for. If you cannot find any of the spices listed in a recipe, try using the curry powder with the sauce. Asafetida (a tree resin), turmeric, cumin and fresh ginger, which are listed below all aid digestion.

4 fl oz (110ml) cooking oil
1 medium onion, chopped
1lb (450g) fresh tomatoes, blanched, peeled and chopped
2 inch cube fresh ginger, peeled and chopped
4 cloves garlic, peeled
1 teaspoon black mustard seeds
1/2 teaspoon cumin seeds
1/4 teaspoon asafetida, powdered
3/4 teaspoon turmeric powder
1 teaspoon coriander powder
1 tablespoon cumin powder

Put the tomatoes, onions, ginger and garlic into a blender and blend to a smooth paste. Heat the oil in a large and heavy bottomed frying pan. Throw in the black mustard seeds and when they stop popping quickly add the cumin seeds and the asafetida and remove the pan from the heat. Immediately pour in the blended mixture, which will begin to splutter when it makes contact with the hot oil. Quickly stir the mixture from side to side to prevent it from burning. Return the pan to low heat and add all the spices. Stir frequently and cook until all the water has evaporated and the oil begins to separate from the mixture. If preferred some of the oil may be spooned out.

MAIN COURSES

Chickpea Curry

Pesto with Fusilli, Roasted Peppers & Aubergines

Handwa - Fermented Yoghurt Bake

Tofu with Broccoli

Butter Bean Stew

Okra

Chow Mein with Fried Tofu

Indian Stir Fry

Chinese Stir Fry with Tofu & Garlic Ginger Sauce

Four Rice with Mung Bean Sprouts

Spinakopita

Ratatouille

Penne Arrabbiata

Spiced Aubergine

Split Mung Dahl (Lentil)

Turtle Beans with Fresh Coriander

Chickpea Curry

Cultivated chickpeas have been with mankind for so long that their wild form is practically unknown and those "wild" chickpeas of Mesopotamia and Palestine are the escapees from cultivation! Probably a native to Western Asia, from the Middle East they spread to the Mediterranean regions with the Arab traders and to South and Central America with the Portuguese and the Spanish. These days chickpeas, their products and the dishes made from them are available practically anywhere in the world. Names like paella, humus, falafel, cocido, d fenna, daphina, harira, channa, barfi, chowle, couscous and garbanzo to name a few have a ring of universality about them. Chickpeas come in all sizes and colours. Some are whitish, yellow, red, brown and black but all have an easily recognizable shape - like the head of a little chick or a small hazelnut.

Chickpea curry has become one of the favourite dishes at the school. Many students try it at home and wonder why it doesn't come out the same. You cannot overstress that it is important that the chickpeas be cooked until they get really soft and allow some of them to break down. That way they are not only easily digestible but absorb and hold the flavours together. As a matter of fact this is true with all the pulses. (For more information on pulses read the introduction to Butter Bean Stew).

Curry Sauce (see recipe)
14 oz (400 g) chickpeas, soaked overnight
1 teaspoon channa masala if available
or $1/2$ teaspoon garam masala
1-$1^1/2$ teaspoons salt
1 green chilli, finely chopped
or $1/4$ teaspoon chilli powder
1 tablespoon lemon juice (optional)
2 tablespoons fresh coriander, chopped

Drain and rinse the chickpeas. Bring them to a boil in a pressure cooker with twice their volume of water. Remove any froth formed with a strainer. Put the lid and whistle on and cook them under full pressure for about 45 minutes. (They will take longer if not in a pressure cooker). Remove from the heat and wait until the steam settles down. Take the whistle out and allow any residual steam left to escape before opening the lid. To test for doneness press the chickpea between the fingers - it should be soft right through. Mix in the curry sauce, salt and chilli. Include lemon juice if using. Bring to a boil and simmer over low heat for about 15 minutes with the lid on but without the pressure. Check that the sauce has thickened from some of the chickpeas having broken down. If not, press and paste some of them with a spoon against the sides of the pan. Add the channa or garam masala and the fresh coriander before serving with chapatis or rice (see recipe).

Pesto with Fusilli, Roasted Peppers & Aubergines

Serves 4

Pesto with fusilli and fresh vegetables makes for a very fulfilling meal. For information on basil and the pine nuts that are used in making the pesto sauce, read pesto sauce recipe.

for the vegetables
2 medium size aubergines, cut length wise into four,
diced into $1/2$ inch (1.5cm)
2 red peppers, whole
6 - 8 tablespoons olive oil
$1/4$ teaspoon salt

for the pasta
1lb (450g) whole wheat fusilli (spiral) pasta
1 tablespoon salt

Place the diced aubergines and whole peppers on a baking tray lined with grease proof paper. Bake in a preheated oven marked 200°c (400°f) for about 10 - 15 minutes or until aubergines are almost done and the peppers have somewhat shrivelled. Remove from oven. Place the peppers in a plastic bag for a minute and the skins will peel off very easily. Halve them and remove the seeds and cut into $1/2$ x 1 inch (1.25 x 2.5cm). Heat oil in a large frying pan, with salt, sauté them with the aubergines over high heat until browned. Set aside.

Bring to boil 7 pints (4 ltrs) of water with salt in a large pan. Add the pasta, turn heat low, stir the pasta frequently and cook for about 12 minutes until al dente and drain. You may want to rinse the pasta, but in doing so more nutrients and the nutty flavour of the pasta will be washed away. Mix them with the vegetables and the pesto sauce and serve immediately. Serve parmesan on the side if not used in making the pesto sauce.

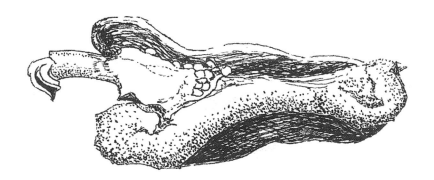

Handwa - Fermented Yoghurt Bake

This dish comes from Northern India. The base of it is lentil and rice flour (handwa) which can be purchased from Indian grocers. If you can't find it use coarse corn meal flour mixed with whole wheat flour. The flour is mixed with yoghurt and allowed to ferment overnight. While baking, the slight sour smell, not unlike sourdough bread, permeates the whole kitchen. This a a very hearty dish and the sourdough bread lovers will definitely like it though the sourness in this dish is quite different. Do not get frightened with the list of ingredients. The dish is actually very simple to make and does not take much time to assemble. Even if you do not have all the spices, try it with what you do have.

6 tablespoons cooking oil

8 oz (225g) handwa flour or

6 oz (175g) coarse corn meal flour with 2 oz (50g) whole wheat flour

1lb 4 oz (560g) yoghurt

2 medium carrots, coarsely grated

4 oz (100g) fresh or frozen peas

1 teaspoon black mustard seeds

1 teaspoon garam masala or curry powder

1^{1}/2 teaspoons baking powder

2 teaspoons fresh ginger, finely chopped

3 tablespoons fresh chopped coriander optional

4 oz (100g) sesame seeds

In a baking casserole 10 x 8 x 2 inch deep (25 x 20 cm x 5 cm deep), mix well the flour with the yoghurt. Cover it with a cling film and keep it in a warm place overnight. Heat the oil until hot. Add black mustard seeds and wait until they stop popping. Take the pan off the heat and immediately add the peas and the carrots stirring constantly. Add all the spices and the salt and stir well before mixing the mixture into the casserole. Sieve over the mixture baking powder and mix making sure to incorporate it well and not leave it trapped or lumped in one area. Stir in the fresh coriander if using. Sprinkle sesame seeds and cover the whole top of the casserole and bake in a preheated oven marked 170°c (325°f) for about 40 - 50 minutes and the sesame seeds have turned brown. Test by inserting a knife in the middle of the casserole to see if cooked. The knife should come out dry or moist but not wet.

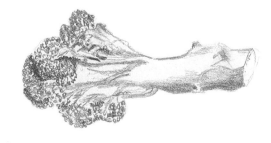

Tofu with Broccoli

Tofu is not very difficult to make at home. In an hour you can make up to 2.5lbs (over one kilo) of tofu. The Soya beans need to be soaked overnight and then blended into a smooth purée. This is then cooked, strained and the derived milk boiled. The milk is then curdled using lemon juice or nigari, a salt derivative from the sea that acts as a coagulant. The curds formed are then strained passing them through cheesecloth and the remains pressed to form tofu. One pounds of Soya beans can yield about 3 - 4 pounds of tofu and at a much cheaper rate than the commercial tofu and when served at its peak of freshness, homemade tofu contains a full flavour and subtle sweetness seldom found in even the finest commercial varieties. Many tofu cookbooks print recipes for home made tofu and are easy to follow. In this recipe tofu is cooked using spices and it lends itself to a different flavour. For more information on tofu and Soya beans, see under tofu pâté, and the Chinese stir-fry with tofu and ginger and garlic sauce recipes.

 4 fl oz (120ml) cooking oil
 1 large onion sliced
 3 cloves garlic finely chopped
 1lb 4 oz (560g) firm tofu drained and absorbed of excess moisture
 and sliced $^1/4$ inch ($^1/2$ cm) thick
 $^1/2$ tablespoon finely chopped ginger
 10 oz (275g) fresh ripe tomatoes finely chopped
 $^1/2$ tablespoon cumin powder
 1 teaspoon coriander powder
 $^3/4$ tablespoon sabji masala, (if not available mild curry powder)
 $^1/2$ teaspoon chilli powder
 $^1/2$ tablespoon salt
 3 x 10 oz (275 g) heads of broccoli cut into mid size florets

Heat oil in a large frying pan preferably non-stick. Add garlic and ginger followed by tofu slices and sauté them over medium heat until brown and crisp. Add the spices and salt, stir briefly and add onions and cook until they turn tender. Add the tomatoes and the broccoli and mix well. Cook covered until broccoli is cooked. This dish is substantial and light and may be eaten on its own or with any grain, pasta or bread.

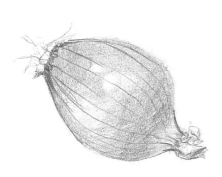

Butter Bean Stew

Contrary to the popular myth, pulses (dried beans, peas and lentils) are filling rather than fattening and contain the lowest fat of any protein foods. They are also rich in vitamins A & B complex. Pulses though are notoriously associated with "wind" and discomfort. If our social customs were to allow for unconditional "windbreaks" surely some relief is bound to be found. While not waiting for such taboos to change, there are some measures that can be taken. Pulses, particularly the hard skinned ones, contain complex sugars called oligosaccharides which arrive intact in large intestines and are not easily broken down by enzymes. Here the friendly bacteria feed on them, releasing carbon dioxide, hydrogen, methane and acids. Soaking pulses removes some of these sugars so always discard soaked water and rinse the pulses before cooking. If you still experience any problems, cover them in cold water and parboil for 5 minutes then drain and rinse properly before the final cooking. Since pulses are rich both in proteins and starches, it is important that they be cooked until soft right through. Never add salt until they have become soft as it toughens their skins. Adding savoury, turmeric, asafoetida, ginger (or a potato before cooking commences and discarding at the end) increases digestibility. Especially for the hard skinned pulses adding kombu helps soften them as does pressure cooking.

> 6 tablespoons olive oil
> 1 large onion, diced
> 2 medium carrots cut into small chunks
> 2 stalks celery chopped into small pieces
> 2 medium courgettes halved and cut into small chunks
> 2 medium red peppers cored and diced
> 1lb (450g) butter beans rinsed and soaked overnight
> 1/2 teaspoon turmeric
> 2 teaspoons medium hot curry powder
> 2 teaspoons cumin powder
> juice of one lemon
> 3 tablespoons fresh chopped coriander

Drain the soaked butter beans and rinse them well. Place them in a medium size pan with twice as much water and cook until some beans begin to break down. Drain and save the water. Meanwhile sauté the onions until transparent. Add the turmeric, cumin, curry powder and salt and cook for a minute. Mix in all the vegetables and cook with the lid on until just tender. Mix them with the beans and along with the saved water, add a total of 2 pints (1ltr) of water. Allow the stew to simmer with the lid on until it really thickens from some of the broken beans to help blend all the flavours together. Add lemon juice and chopped coriander. Serve with rice or eat on its own.

Okra

Okra belongs to the nightshade family and it is no wonder that they go so well with tomatoes. They are green, slim, long and pyramidal five sided capsules. The capsules or the pods are often called ladies' fingers and its botanical name is Hibiscus Estculentus, a native to tropical Africa. When very young and tender the capsules may be eaten raw but are most preferred when cooked. Okra exudes a mucilaginous liquid, which often is used as a thickening and flavouring agent for sauces and soups. Outside of tropical Africa, okras are fairly popular in the Mediterranean region. Recently their popularity has spread to Europe and in particular to England, mostly through the Indian restaurants, where the cooked dish is recognised by the name bhindi. In England, almost every high street has an Indian restaurant and this has become an accepted feature of the British culture. When buying fresh okra, select the ones that are small, tender, green and without any spots on them. Often they can be stringy and if the tip of the okra snaps easily, it is a good sign.

5 fl oz (150ml) cooking oil

1 large onion, sliced

12 oz (350g) fresh chopped tomatoes

1lb 8 oz (700g) okra washed, dried and stalked without damaging the cones

1 teaspoon black mustard seeds

1/2 teaspoon cumin seeds

3/4 tablespoon cumin powder

1/2 teaspoon turmeric

5 cloves or a pinch ground powder

3 x 1 inch (2.5cm) long cinnamon stick, hard variety, or a 1/4 teaspoon ground powder

1 teaspoon salt

1 green chilli, seeded and finely chopped optional

or 1/4 teaspoon chilli powder, optional

In a large bottomed pan or a frying pan, preferably non-stick, heat the oil until hot and add the black mustard seeds and wait until they start popping. When they stop popping, quickly add the cumin seeds followed immediately by the onions and reduce the heat to low and cook the onions until transparent. Mix in the spices and the salt with the onions and cook for a minute before adding the tomatoes. Cook for five more minutes with the lid off. Add the okra and cook them with the lid on to allow them to cook in their own steam. Stir them frequently until they are cooked. Stir them gently otherwise the pods will open and make the dish rather sticky. Serve with rice or chapatis or bread. (See the recipe).

Chow Mein with Fried Tofu *Serves 4*

W Shurtleff & A Aoyagi, in their book of tofu, propose two theories that could account for the discovery of tofu. One is that by adding natural salt which contains nigari as a flavouring to puréed soya beans would have curdled it and consequently formed curds. Removing the fibrous okara from the purée and pressing the resultant curds would have given what we call tofu. Secondly, since Chinese did not generally raise cows or goats for milk, they were unfamiliar with the curdling process and that the idea was imported from the Indians in the south or the Mongols in the north.

The flavour derived in the following tofu dish is through browning garlic and ginger and when used with soya sauce, gives a distinct taste. As for chow mein, it has an aromatic and nutty flavour, which comes from using toasted sesame oil.

14 oz (400g) firm tofu drained, excess moisture absorbed, cut into
2 x 2 inch (5 x 5cm) square and $1/4$ inch thick slices
6 tablespoons toasted sesame oil
4 tablespoons cooking oil
1 medium onion thinly sliced
2 small carrots cut lengthwise into halves and thinly sliced diagonally
2 sticks celery thinly sliced diagonally
2 oz (50g) bean sprouts, rinsed
2 medium courgettes cut lengthwise and thinly sliced diagonally
2 small red peppers sliced in thin strips
4 tablespoons soya sauce
$1^{1}/2$ tablespoons salt for cooking noodles, vegetables and tofu
4 cloves garlic, finely chopped
2 tablespoons fresh ginger, finely chopped, for tofu and the noodles
15 oz (425g) Chinese egg noodles broken into small pieces

Heat cooking oil in a large frying pan preferably non-stick. Add garlic and 1 tablespoon of ginger and fry until they brown. Add tofu, sprinkle $1/2$ teaspoon salt and fry them over medium heat until brown and crisp on both sides. Add 2 tablespoons of soya sauce and after a while turn the tofu slices over. Wait until all the soya sauce has been absorbed.

Heat three tablespoons of sesame oil in a large wok and over medium heat fry the onions. Add in succession salt, carrots, celery, peppers, courgettes, bean sprouts and mange touts stiring constantly until vegetables are crisp, brown and tender. Add 2 tablespoons of soya sauce, mix well and set aside.

In a large pan bring 8 pts (4 ltrs) of water to a boil. Add 1 tablespoon salt and cook the egg noodles according to the instructions on the packet. To retain the full flavour of the noodles do not rinse them after cooked. When done, drain and immediately heat 3 tablespoons of sesame oil and fry the ginger for a while taking care not to burn it. Add the egg noodles and the soya sauce and mix well. Mix it with the vegetables and serve with tofu on the side.

Indian Stir Fry

4 fl oz (120 ml) cooking oil
1 teaspoon black mustard seeds
$1/2$ teaspoon black cumin seeds if available (or normal cumin seeds)
1 small onion, sliced
10 oz (275 g) bean sprouts, rinsed
4 oz (110g) mange tout, sliced diagonally
1lb 14 oz (850g) cauliflower, cut into small florets
2 small courgettes, halved and sliced diagonally
4 oz (110g) French beans, sliced diagonally
$3/4$ teaspoon turmeric
2 teaspoons cumin powder
$3/4$ tablespoon medium hot curry powder
A few curry leaves, optional
3 tablespoons fresh coriander, finely chopped
4 oz (110g) almonds, roasted and chopped
4 oz (110g) cashews, roasted and chopped

Roast the nuts in a preheated oven at 170°c (325°f) for about 15 minutes. Allow to cool, and chop. Set aside.

In a wok heat oil until hot, add black mustard seeds and wait for them to pop. When they stop popping, quickly add the cumin seeds followed by the onion. Remove from the heat and stir the onions from side to side to prevent them from burning. Return the wok to a low heat and cook the onions until they are brown. Stir in the spices, curry leaves and salt and cook for a minute. Add the cauliflower and the French beans and after five minutes add the rest of the vegetables and 12 fl oz (300 ml) water. Cover and cook until the vegetables are just tender. Before serving, sprinkle the nuts and fresh coriander over the vegetables. Serve with rice (see recipe).

Chinese Stir Fry with Tofu & Garlic Ginger Sauce

Chinese-style firm tofu or Japanese-style momen goshi (cotton filtered) or kinu-goshi (silken tofu) are best known and most popular types. The former is good for stir fries, sautés and spreads. The latter type has a delicate texture and flavour and is used for desserts and fruit whips. In Japan and China there has been a close link between tofu and Buddhist related activities. Bodhidharma, who lived in China between 520 and 528, and who founded the Chinese Zen school, is said to have engaged tofu in "Dharma Combat" to probe tofu's understanding of the Buddha's way. Bodhidharma later praised tofu for its simplicity, its honest straightforward nature and its lovely white robes. It is thought that Buddhist monks took tofu from China to Japan around the 8th century. All the large Chinese and Japanese temples and monasteries had within them the earliest tofu shops run by Buddhist priests and temple cooks. The major Kamakura Zen temples opened Buddhist vegetarian restaurants within the temple compounds, which had tofu on their menus.

   5 tablespoons toasted sesame oil

   $3^1/2$ fl oz (100 ml) soya sauce

   1lb 4 oz (560 g) firm tofu, drained and cut into small cubes

   1 tablespoon corn starch

   1 small onion, thinly sliced

   2 medium size carrots, peeled, halved and thinly sliced

   12 oz (350 g) cauliflower, cut into small florets

   2 small courgettes, halved and thinly sliced

   4 cloves of garlic, finely chopped

   1 tablespoon fresh ginger, finely grated

   6 oz (175 g) unhulled toasted sesame seeds

In a heavy frying pan over low heat, toast sesame seeds until lightly browned. Blend them coarsely in a coffee grinder and set aside. In a flat dish marinate tofu with 3 tablespoons of soya sauce and ginger for 2 hours.

In a medium size pan, with one tablespoon of oil, fry garlic until it is nicely browned. Add 2 pints (1 litre) of of boiling water. Mix the corn starch with soya sauce in a small bowl, add to the water and mix with a wire whisk until it begins to boil and thicken. Add the tofu pieces with ginger and bring to a boil again. Set aside.

Pour 4 tablespoons of oil into a large wok and stir fry the onions over a medium heat followed by the rest of the vegetable in the order that they appear in the recipe. Leave about 30 seconds between each kind of vegetable and cook them until they become tender. Turn the heat to high and, stirring constantly, allow them to brown a little. Pour the sauce with the tofu over the vegetables and bring to a boil. Serve with rice or quinoa (see recipe). Sprinkle the toasted sesame seeds over each serving.

Four Rice with Mung Bean Sprouts

Rice has been cultivated in China for over 5000 years and for a long time on the foot hills of the Himalayas. Around 400 BC Theophrastus mentions its cultivation in India. Rice was brought to Europe by Alexander the Great. There are altogether 2400 varieties of cultivated rice and in India alone about 1100 of those are cultivated. Rice is the only cereal that is cultivated in flooded fields which remain flooded for the major part of the growing season and are normally drained some weeks before harvest. There are however varieties of rice that grow in soil that is not flooded. Such rice is called dry, upland or hill rice and is the oldest cultivated form but today is without economic importance. Wild rice grows in Africa and S E Asia, and N America is in fact a place of another genus, but belongs to the same group. Wild rice was an important cereal for the American Indians, although it is strictly not a cultivated grass. The best basmati rice grows on the foothills of the Himalayas in both India and Pakistan. In its natural state it is brown and when polished it becomes white. When cooked after a year of its cultivation, it becomes less sticky and also improves its nutty aroma.

In this recipe, wild rice is combined with the other three rices and sprouted mung beans and the blend yields to an interesting texture and unusual, nutty and full bodied flavour.

To relish it, do not mix it with any accompanied dish but rather serve it on the side. May be served with mushroom sauce or ratatouille. (See recipe).

- 3 oz (75g) wild rice rinsed
- 3 oz (75g) red rice rinsed
- 3 oz (75g) brown basmati rice rinsed
- 3 oz (75) white basmati rice rinsed
- 4 oz (110g) mung beans to sprout
- 5 fl oz (150ml) olive oil
- 1 teaspoon salt

To sprout mung beans soak them in warm water for about 6 hours. Rinse, drain and place them in a large glass jar by a sunny window sill or a warm place. Rinse and drain twice a day with hand warm water and return the jar to window sill. In 2 -3 days the sprouts will be ready. Rinse and set aside.

To cook the rice, bring 1 3/4 pt (1 ltr) water to a boil in a medium size deep rather than wide pan, and along with the salt add wild and red rices to the boiling water. Bring the water to a boil again, cover and let it simmer for 20 minutes. Rinse, and add brown basmati rice, bring to boil, cover and let it simmer for another 15 minutes. Repeat the process with white basmati rice and cook for 20 more minutes. Add more water if required. The rice should come out nice and fluffy.

Heat the olive oil in a large frying pan. Add and sauté the mung beans until tender. Add the rice and mix in well.

Spinakopita

Named after the Greek word for 'leaf', filo is a versatile pastry with a history that is believed to go back thousands of years. At one time this pastry was available only in Greek or oriental stores but now most large supermarkets carry them and it is available either fresh or frozen. Apart from its suitability for a wide range of sweet or savoury dishes, filo pastry's appeal has in its unique crispy texture, fried or baked, and it does not use much fat during its making or while preparing a dish. Because the pastry is very thin, it requires a little extra care in its handling. All the manufacturers carry on their packet instructions that are easy to follow.

2 tablespoons olive oil

4 oz (110 g) chopped spring onions or 1 medium onion finely chopped

1 lb (450 g) fresh spinach, stalked, steamed, drained and finely chopped (frozen may be used)

8 oz (225 g) feta cheese, crumbled

4 eggs lightly beaten

2 tablespoons fresh parsley chopped

1 teaspoon freshly grated nutmeg

1 teaspoon salt

1/4 teaspoon pepper

1lb (450 g) fresh or frozen filo pastry (12 sheets)

Approx 3 oz (75g) melted butter or oil for assembling pie

Heat oil in a medium pan and sauté spring onions until just done and allow them to cool. Mix in spinach followed by the cheese, eggs and all the seasonings. Grease a baking tray size 14 x 10 inches (35 x 24cm). Line the tray with six sheets of filo pastry brushing each with butter or oil. Spread the mixture evenly leaving approx 1/4 inch (1/2 cm) borders all around. Fold the borders over the filling. Cut the remaining sheets leaving them long enough to tuck down and place them over the mixture brushing each with butter or oil. Brush the top with butter or oil and lightly score the top layers of the pastry with a sharp knife. Sprinkle water to prevent pastry from curling. Bake in a preheated oven marked 180°c (350°f) for about 30 - 40 minutes. Wait for five minutes before cutting.

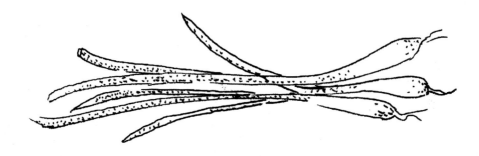

Ratatouille

Ratatouille is very popular in France, particularly in the south. The climate there is very suitable for the vegetables and the herb used in this recipe. Aubergines, onions, peppers and courgettes are individually sautéd until just tender and slightly browned. The tomatoes are then added to this composite which then is cooked in an oven. The result of all the juices releasing from different vegetables and the thyme gives this dish a special flavour of the province.

olive oil to sauté vegetables
1 large onion, sliced
2 medium aubergines, quartered lengthwise and diced into $^1/_2$ inch (1.5cm)
2 bell peppers, diced the same size as the aubergines
3 medium size courgettes, halved and diced as the aubergines
1 teaspoon salt
$^1/_4$ teaspoon black pepper
1 teaspoon dry thyme
1lb 4 oz (560 g) fresh ripe tomatoes, chopped

In a large frying pan, except for the tomatoes, sauté each vegetable separately until just tender and browned. Transfer them to an ovenproof casserole, sprinkle salt, thyme and add the tomatoes. In a preheated oven marked 170°c (325°f) cook the casserole with a lid on for about 40 - 50 minutes. Two or three times, while the casserole is baking, gently turn the vegetables around. Cook until the juices turn syrupy and the vegetables have a somewhat glossy look. Eat hot with rice or pasta or as a cold salad.

Penne Arrabbiata

For the ingredients and the method for Pomarola tomato sauce (see recipe)

> 2 tablespoons olive oil
> 2 green bell peppers, seeded and cut in $1/2$ inch (1cm) strips
> 2 cloves garlic, finely chopped
> 1 seeded green chilli finely chopped or $1/2$ teaspoon dried hot pepper flakes
> 6 oz (175g) freshly grated Parmesan cheese
> 1lb (450g) penne
> few fresh basil leaves, chopped
> 1 tablespoon salt for cooking pasta

There are many versions of cooking penne arrabbiata. This recipe uses the pomarola tomato sauce, combined with pasta, green peppers, parmesan cheese and some chilli.

Make the pomarola sauce as per the recipe.

Heat oil in a medium pan and sauté the green bell peppers until tender. Add garlic and the chilli and cook for a moment. Mix in the pomarola tomato sauce and cook further for a couple of minutes.

In a large pot bring 7 pts (4 1trs) of water with salt to a rolling boil. Add penne and bring water to a boil again. Reduce heat to low and continue to cook stirring frequently until al dente, approx 12 minutes. Drain and mix it with the sauce. Garnish with fresh basil and serve immediately with the parmesan on the side.

Spiced Aubergine

Aubergine or eggplant as it is popularly known is unfortunately a misleading name. Only the primitive varieties from Thailand are round and small and somewhat resemble eggs. The varieties come in different shapes and sizes. Some are very long, slender and snake-like. Others are oblong, oval, sausage-like, thin, dwarf and pumpkin shaped. In colour there are equally as many shades. The dark, deep satiny purple is the most common one sold in the west. Then there are the purplish red, greenish white, greenish yellow and an amazing ivory white. Aubergines belong to the nightshade family and marry well with tomatoes. They are very versatile and are used as a pâté, roasted, baked, fried and stuffed. The aubergines used in this recipe are the most common variety and in my experience I have yet to come across one that is bitter. Aubergines soak up oil like blotting paper and to reduce this effect, precooking them in an oven seems to help.

> Basic curry sauce (see recipe)
> 1lb 8oz (700g) aubergines
> 3/4 teaspoon fennel seeds
> 1/2 teaspoon garam masala
> 1 teaspoon salt
> fresh coriander for garnish

Quarter the aubergines lengthwise and cut into cubes. If you do not wish to precook them in the oven, skip the next step. Bake them in a preheated oven mark 200°c (400°f) for about 15 minutes until they brown.

Heat the oil in a deep, large and heavy frying pan, preferably non-stick, and sauté the fennel seeds until they brown slightly. Add the curry sauce, heating up if cold, and add the aubergines and the salt. Cover and mix gently and frequently until cooked. Stir in the garam masala. Garnish with fresh coriander and serve with rice or pooris (see recipe).

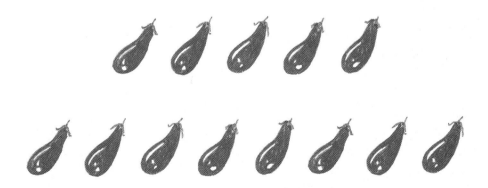

Split Mung Dahl (Lentil)

Serves 6

Archaeological evidence suggests that pulses were amongst the earliest crops to be cultivated. Found in excavations, peas have been carbon dated beyond 9000 BC and in Peru lima beans have been found dating from 4000-5000 BC. Lentils have been found in Egyptian tombs and they have also been mentioned in the Bible. It is interesting to see how the names were given to things from their association with the pulses. For example, when the glass lens was discovered, it was named after the lentil due to its similar shape. The carat bean is responsible for the jeweller's carat. Due to the carat bean's uniformity, they were used, and still are in some countries, for weighing gold. Of all the lentils, mung dahl is the most easily digestible. According to Ayurveda, the ancient Indian medicine, mung dahl plus rice is recommended when a person is recovering from an illness. What we see in Chinese stir fries as bean sprouts are the mung beans unsprouted. When split and their green skins are removed, they are called mung dahl (lentils). For more information on pulses see the Butter Bean Stew recipe.

curry Sauce (see recipe)
6 oz (175g) mung dahl, washed and soaked
1 green chilli, chopped very finely or $^1/4$ teaspoon red chilli powder
$^1/2$ teaspoon dahl masala (optional)
1 teaspoon salt
1 tablespoon fresh coriander, chopped
A few curry leaves (optional)

Soak the mung dahl for an hour in warm water. Drain and rinse thoroughly. In a medium sized pan without the lid, bring the dahl to the boil.

Spoon out any froth that forms. Add the curry sauce, salt, curry leaves and the fresh or dry chilli and cook until the dahl is tender. The consistency of the dahl should be neither too thick nor too thin. Add dahl masala if using, and garnish with fresh coriander before serving. When served with rice, pour enough dahl over it as the rice will quickly absorb it and dilute its flavour.

The Krishnamurti Centre lounge and library.

Turtle Beans with Fresh Coriander *Serves 4-6*

Since beans have been with mankind for a long time, it is not surprising that the mention of their name appears in different contexts of life - from the political to the social. Both the Romans and Greeks used beans for casting votes when electing people for public office. Apparently Pythagoras forbade his pupils from having beans which meant to keep away from politics! Aristotle would advise his pupils to abstain from beans, which meant from sexual indulgence. In either case it had nothing to do with dietary restrictions, as one might think! In the late 1800s to say 'I haven't got a bean' meant one didn't have any money or 'to spill the beans' meant to give away a secret. We are all familiar with the saying 'full of beans' or an 'old bean' meaning good friend. In Japan and China references to tofu, which is a product of soy beans, are also made. In China finding fault with a person is compared to 'finding a bone in your tofu'. In Japan, to say 'it's as futile as trying to clamp two pieces of tofu together' indicates something as being completely hopeless. Navy beans are small blackish-blue beans that are very popular in Brazil and are eaten with rice. They are succulent and absorb the flavours well. They bleed an amazingly dark purplish-black colour when soaked and continue to do so while cooking. For more information on pulses read the introduction to the recipe for Butter Bean Stew.

    6 tablespoons olive oil
    1 small onion, finely chopped
    2 small carrots, diced in small pieces
    2 celery sticks, diced in small pieces
    2 medium courgettes, diced in small pieces
    5 oz (150 g) button mushrooms, diced into small pieces
    10 oz (275 g) turtle beans, soaked for at least 6 hours in warm water
    1 tablespoon mild curry powder
    1/2 tablespoon cumin powder
    1 teaspoon salt
    4 tablespoons fresh coriander, chopped

Drain and rinse the beans thoroughly. In a medium sized pan, bring them to a boil with twice as much water. If a froth forms, scoop it off with a strainer. Reduce heat, put the lid on and allow to simmer until some of the beans begin to break, then set aside. Meanwhile heat oil in a frying pan over a low heat and sauté the onions until the they are transparent. Stir in salt, cumin and curry powder and cook for half a minute. Add the rest of the vegetables and sauté for 10 more minutes. Mix them with the beans along with the saved water. Cook the mixture for a while until the stew begins to thicken from some of the broken beans. To have enough sauce to use with rice, add extra water if required. Stir in the fresh coriander before serving.

DESSERTS

Cream Caramel

Saffron Rice Pudding

Rosewater & Yoghurt Cake

Pear Cake

Shikhand

Mango Cream

Tarte En Bande

Chocolate Mousse with Grand Marnier

Apple & Nuts in Filo Pastry (Filo Wrap)

Mille-Feuilles

Marzipan Pears in Pâté Sucree

Fruit Salad with Rosewater & Yoghurt

Prune Mousse with Yoghurt

Almond Cake

Apple Crumble

Cream Caramel

for the syrup

1 1/2 tablespoons caster sugar

3 tablespoons water

6 small ramekins 1 1/2 by 3 inch deep (3.5 x 7.5cm)

or a glass bowl, capacity 1 3/4 pt (1ltr)

In a small pan, cook the sugar and the water until it turns into a golden syrup and begins to darken. Pour the caramel syrup into the ramekins and allow it to set. If using the glass bowl use only 3/4 of the caramel syrup.

for the cream

a scant pint - 500 ml milk

4 oz (110g) caster sugar

3 large eggs

1 teaspoon vanilla

In a medium pan, bring milk to boil. In a large bowl, whisk the eggs, sugar and vanilla essence. Pour a little of the boiling milk over the mixture and whisk quickly to prevent eggs from cooking. Pour the mixture back into the remaining of the milk and whisk again. Fill up the ramekins with the mixture, or the bowl if using it instead.

Fold a tea towel in three and place it into 1 inch (2.5cm) deep tray. Fill it up to 1/2 inch (1.25cm) with the cold water and place the ramekins over the tea towel to prevent the cream from boiling while cooking in the oven. Put the tray in a preheated oven marked 170°c (325°f) for about 20 minutes or until set, in the case of the bowl approx 30 - 40 mins. Allow them to cool a little and place them in the refrigerator until chilled. Run a knife along the circumference of the ramekins and move the cream caramel a little with your fingers to dislodge it if stuck. Place the serving plate over the top of the ramekin and turn it upside down to allow the cream caramel to slide onto the plate and then lift off the ramekin. Serve them upside down with the caramel running down the sides of the creams.

Saffron Rice Pudding

If you had been raised in a country where there is a tradition of having rice milk pudding regularly in your home and you had resisted eating it, try this one for a change. The first time this pudding was served at Brockwood, it was done so under a pseudonym lest it arouse the memories of the horror of the 'eat your pudding' syndrome associated with boarding school.

Saffron has been considered to be one of the most expensive spices. Since only the stigmata of a crocus flower is picked by hand, the process is very labour intensive. But do not be deterred by the price since using only a little goes a long way. The expensiveness of saffron led to frequent adulteration of it. It is recorded that in 1444 a citizen of Nuremberg by the name of Findeker was burned alive for adulteration of saffron and in 1456 a woman called Ellis Pfragnerin was buried alive for the same offence! During this period, weight for weight saffron was more expensive than gold. For centuries saffron had been used as a medicine, as a perfume and as a dye. Now it is mostly used for cooking and food dye purposes. Though a native to the Eastern Mediterranean region, it is cultivated in Europe, India and China. The name saffron originates from the Arabic zafaran meaning yellow.

> 5-6 oz (150-175g) pudding rice (if available)
> 4 pints (1.8 litres) whole milk
> 4-5 oz (110-150g) sugar
> or 6 oz (175g) acacia honey
> $1^1/2$ teaspoon coarsely ground cardamom
> 1 large pinch saffron
> 4 oz (110g) roasted chopped almonds

In a medium size heavy bottomed pan, bring milk to a boil over a medium heat while stirring frequently. Add the rice and sugar or the honey. Stir making sure the milk does not scald and bring it to a boil again. Reduce the heat then let it simmer with the lid off. Continue to stir frequently until the pudding begins to thicken and the milk is reduced to almost half. The whole process should take about an hour. The pudding should have the consistency of a thickish runny porridge. Add the cardamom and the saffron at the end and blend them well. Allow the pudding to cool and then chill. Wait at least two hours before serving. The flavour really develops if the pudding is left for a day and lovely yellow colour permeates the whole pudding. It can be served hot but tastes better when chilled. Serve with toasted chopped almonds sprinkled on top.

Rosewater & Yoghurt Cake

This recipe originates from Iran. Rosewater can be purchased from oriental grocers or from chemists. Check for the expiry date, as the strength of the scent and the flavour does tend to fade with age and can also vary from one manufacturer to another. If you use the concentrated type, you will require a few drops to a teaspoon for the same recipe. The cake is very thin and comes out a little chewy.

4 oz (110g) plain flour

1^1/2 teaspoons baking powder

4 oz (110g) caster sugar

8 oz (225g) tart yoghurt

1 lemon rind, finely grated

2 tablespoons lemon juice (optional, to add tartness to yoghurt)

4 tablespoons cooking oil

2 eggs

A few drops of concentrated rosewater (or as required)

plus more for the cream (optional)

5 fl oz (150 ml) whipping cream, whipped (optional)

2 tablespoons icing sugar

In a large bowl lightly beat the sugar, eggs and oil until all the sugar dissolves. Add the yoghurt, rosewater, lemon rind and juice if using and blend with a wire whisk until smooth. Taste and add more rosewater if required. Be careful not to use too much as it can overpower the cake. Grease a shallow roasting tray (size 16"x10"/40x25cm) and line with greaseproof paper. Pour in the mixture and it will line the tray in a thin layer. Bake in a preheated oven mark 180°c (350°f) for about 20-30 minutes until the cake is cooked and golden brown. After five minutes turn it out onto a wire rack.

If serving with cream, whip the cream with icing sugar and a few drops of rosewater.

Pear Cake

There is hardly any fat used in this cake. The pear gives an unusual taste and texture to the cake. Pears may be substituted with apples. The fruit of the pear tree, is a pome like the apple or quince. The tree is native to Europe and western Asia, where the wild pear is still found. The pear was mentioned by Homer and the ancient Romans already recognised many kinds of pears. France is the largest producer of pears. 'Doyenne du Comice' and 'Jargonelle' are the oldest cultivated varieties and make excellent eaters while Belissime d'Hiver, St Germain, Catillac and Black Worcester are excellent for stewing. Pears have never achieved the popularity of apples, mainly because they cannot be stored for such a long period. Anatomically, pears differ from apples by the presence of sclereids appearing in small groups, which give the pear a special granular texture.

    5 oz (150g) self raising flour
    9 oz (250g) caster sugar
    3 eggs
    2 tablespoons oil
    2 teaspoons vanilla essence
    1lb 14oz (850g) firm pears, peeled and cut into 1 inch (2.5cm) pieces

In a large bowl beat eggs and sugar with a wire whisk until sugar begins to dissolve. Add flour, oil, vanilla essence and sugar and mix well. Mix in the cut pears and pour the mixture into a greased and lined with grease proof paper baking tin size 9 x 9 inch (22.5 x 22.5cm). Bake the cake in a preheated oven marked 170°c (325°f) for about 30 minutes. Check the middle of the cake with a knife and if it comes out dry, it is done. Let it cool in the tin for five minutes, run a knife along the edges and then turn it onto a wire rack and pull off the paper gently, allowing the cake to cool completely. Serve it upside down, the pears sitting at the bottom makes a lovely pattern.

Shikhand

The aroma of the cardamom and the smoked flavour of the saffron combined give this simple dessert a surprisingly subtle and delicate flavour. If using honey, use acacia as it is flavourless and doesn't clash with cardamom or saffron. Using honey will nonetheless make the dessert thinner and if a thicker consistency is desired mix in about 125g ground almond. Shrikhand is traditionally made by hanging the home made yoghurt in a muslin cloth and allowing it to drip overnight. You need not do that if you use the Greek style yoghurt.

> 2 lb 2 oz (1kg) thick Greek style yoghurt
> 7 oz (200g) caster sugar or 10 oz (275g) honey
> 4 oz (110g) ground almond if using honey
> 1^{1}/$_{2}$ teaspoons cardamom without the skins, coarsely ground
> a few strands of saffron
> 2 oz (50g) toasted almond flakes

Mix yoghurt and sugar with a spoon until all the sugar is dissolved. Add cardamom and saffron and mix well. Stir occasionally to blend the flavours and the colour released by the spices. For the best result, leave in the fridge for a day or at least two hours if in a hurry.

If the saffron is fresh and well stored in a cool place or a fridge, you will need only a few strands. The end result will yield a pale yellow colour to the dessert. Garnish with almond flakes.

Mango Cream

Mangoes come in hundreds of varieties with different sizes, shapes and shades. Some are long and thin, some fat and round, some big and oval and others small. The different shades of colours vary from dark green and dark reddish yellow to reddish purple to mention a few. The unripe mangoes are used for pickles and chutneys. The ripe ones are used for ice creams, sorbets, jams and jellies. They are also canned as pulp and as pieces with syrup and above all they are eaten as a fruit.

Fresh Alfonso mangoes are used in this recipe. They are grown in India and in England they can be bought from Indian grocers in the months of May and June. A visiting friend from India was shocked to see these mangoes sold at a cheaper price and of a far superior quality than are available in India! These are modern times in which we live with their complicated economic systems. Of the canned pulp varieties, Alphonso seems to be the best.

If there were only one item you were allowed to have cream with, for me it would have to be the mango. It adds something to the fruit without taking anything away from it.

    1lb 14oz (850g) fresh mango, peeled and the pulp separated
    (about 6 mangoes will yield this much pulp)
    or 1lb 14oz (850g) mango pulp, canned
    3 fl oz (75 ml) fresh double cream or 6 fl oz (150 ml) yoghurt

Whip the cream and blend in with the mango pulp. If using yoghurt, mix it with the pulp and blend with a wire whisk. Serve chilled.

Tarte En Bande

10 oz (275 g) puff pastry at room temperature
1 pt (570ml) milk
5 oz (150 g) sugar
2 oz (50 g) flour plus little extra for dusting
4 eggs
2 teaspoons vanilla essence
1lb (450g) fresh strawberries washed & dried

Puff pastry used in this dessert can be made at home and making it can be very rewarding if you have the time and the patience. These days many health shops and most supermarkets sell it, it comes either fresh or frozen. For storage and handling read the instructions on the packet. Any fresh fruit can be used in this recipe.

Dust the work surface generously with flour and roll the pastry just a little longer and wider than desired 12 x 4$^{1}/_{2}$ inches 30 x 11.5cm. Cut it to this size with a sharp knife. Lengthwise, cut two strips $^{1}/_{2}$ inch (1.25cm) wide and set aside. Sprinkle water over the baking tray and with the help of the rolling pin, lift the pastry and unroll it over the tray. Brush with water a $^{1}/_{2}$ inch strip along each length of the pastry. Place the cut strips over it and pat them very gently so they remain in place. With a fork prick the whole assembled pastry. In a preheated oven marked 220°c (425°f) bake the pastry for about 20 - 30 mins until well risen and lightly browned. Remove the pastry from the oven and allow it to cool completely. Flatten the risen pastry in the space between the strips to make room for the cream filling. Bring the milk to the boil in a medium size pan. In a bowl whisk sugar, eggs, and vanilla essence. Add and whisk in the flour into a smooth paste.

Add a little of the boiled milk to the mixture and whisk quickly to prevent the eggs from cooking and return it to the rest of the milk. Cook the mixture for about ten minutes whisking constantly to prevent the cream burning or forming lumps. Allow it to cool and then chill it in the refrigerator. Fill the pastry between the strips and arrange the fruit on top. Both the pastry and the cream can be prepared a day ahead. Cut the pastry carefully with a sharp bread knife into slices.

Chocolate Mousse with Grand Marnier   *Serves 6 - 8*

Chocolate has been called the 'food of the gods' and it is one of the most popular foods all over the world. The Cocoa tree, theobroma cacoa, is a native to the tropical slopes of the Andes, and was discovered by Cortez in 1519. If only he had known that he would be making many a longing and lonely heart happy! The cocoa tree was introduced into Ghana, West Africa in 1879 and Ghana remains one of the largest exporters of cocoa seeds. Cocoa seeds were already introduced into Europe by 1526. For the next 300 years they were used only for the production of chocolate drinks. Then a Dutchman extracted the solid fat known today as cocoa butter from the cocoa seeds. This diminished the richness of the chocolate drink and left behind what is known today as the cocoa drink, a de-fatted chocolate. The extracted cocoa butter had no special use for a number of years until solid chocolate was invented. The invention of chocolate mixed with milk was the work of a Swiss man, which was further refined by Lindt, another Swiss man. No wonder Swiss chocolate remains one of the finest today.

5 oz (150 g) dark bitter chocolate
2 oz (50 g) butter
2 oz (50 g) caster sugar
10 fl oz (250ml) whipping cream
4 eggs, separated
1 fl oz (25ml) Grand Marnier
1 teaspoon instant coffee

Melt the butter in a medium size pan over very low heat, add chocolate pieces and whisk until they melt and the mixture is smooth. Allow it to cool and pour in the whipping cream, instant coffee and the Grand Marnier.

Add the egg yolks and blend them in (use only half the egg yolks if a lighter mousse is desired). With an electric beater, whisk the egg whites in a large bowl. Add sugar when the egg whites are almost stiff and continue to beat until they are firm and smooth. Fold them gently in with the mixture. Chill before serving.

Apple & Nuts in Filo Pastry (Filo Wrap)

With a large orchard of cooking apples growing at Brockwood, huge quantities are collected every year and are put to use in many desserts. Any dessert with apple means an immediate association on everyone's part living at Brockwood of many hours spent collecting them in the autumn. They are either picked directly from the trees or from the ground having been caused to fall by the fair share of the winds and the rains we get here. Then there is the coming together of people around the table in the kitchen, often breaking into spontaneous singing, a harvest time of sorts. The apples are washed, cored and chopped before they are finally cooked. The entire surplus of the cooked apples is stored away in large containers in the freezer for later use. Often students who left long ago would write asking for a particular apple recipe. In this recipe the apples are combined with dates eliminating use of any sugar.

makes about 30

2 lbs 8 oz (1kg 125 g) cooking apples peeled and cored
4 oz (110 g) dates, cooked and pitted
5 oz (150 g) hazelnuts roasted, half ground half chopped
2 teaspoons cinnamon
14 oz (400 g) filo pastry
4 oz (110 g) butter or oil

Cook the apples on medium heat without adding any water and with the lid off until the apples are cooked and all their natural water is evaporated. Add the dates, hazelnuts and cinnamon. Allow the mixture to cool. The mixture should be dry. If not, add a little more ground hazelnuts.

Cut the pastry into five inch strips (handle the pastry according to the instructions on the packet). Brush with butter or oil a strip of pastry, fold in half lengthwise and brush again. Place a heaped teaspoon of the filling on end of a strip towards you and fold it into a triangle handling it lightly with each fold. Place the finished triangles on a baking tray and brush them with the rest of the butter or oil. Place the sealed end on the tray. Bake at 180°c (350°f) for about 30 - 40 minutes until golden brown and crisp.

Mille-Feuilles

The pastry used in this recipe is the same as the one used in Tarte en Bande. It can be made at home which can be rewarding if you have the time and patience. These days many health shops and most supermarkets sell it. It comes either fresh or frozen. For storage and handling read the instructions on the packet. This dessert has a delicious home made custard-cream filling and a pretty finish which children particularly like.

> 3 x 10 oz (275 g) puff pastry at room temperature
> 1 pint ($1/2$ litre) milk
> 5 oz (150 g) caster sugar
> 2 large eggs
> $1^1/2$ teaspoon vanilla essence
> 2 oz (50 g) plain flour
> 1 small egg white
> 4-6 tablespoons icing sugar
> 2 oz (50 g) dark cooking chocolate

Dust the work surface generously with flour and roll three rectangles of pastry just a little longer and wider than the desired 12" x $4^1/2$" (30cm x 11.5cm). Cut them to this size with a sharp knife. Sprinkle water over the baking tray and with the help of the rolling pin, lift the rectangles and unroll them onto the tray. Place them next to each other or on separate trays if there is not enough room. Prick the pastries with a fork and bake in a preheated oven mark 220°c (425°f) for about 20-30 minutes until well risen and browned. Remove them from the oven and allow them to cool completely. Flatten the risen pastries gently.

To make the custard cream, bring the milk to a boil in a medium size pan. In a bowl whisk sugar, eggs and vanilla essence. Add the flour and whisk to a smooth paste.

Add a little of the boiled milk to the mixture and whisk quickly to prevent the eggs from cooking and return it to the rest of the milk. Cook the mixture for about ten minutes, whisking constantly to prevent the cream burning or forming lumps. Allow it to cool and then chill it in the refrigerator. Spread a little of the cream over one rectangle of pastry. Place the second rectangle over the cream and repeat, ending by placing the third piece of pastry on top of the other two with the smooth side facing up.

Mix the egg white with icing sugar until the mixture becomes thick and spreadable but not a paste. Spread it over the top with a table knife.

Make a piping bag using a small cone shaped funnel of greaseproof paper. Cut a small hole at the bottom with a pair of scissors. Melt the chocolate in a double boiler. Pour it into the funnel while pinching the hole shut. Release the hole and squeeze out thin lines $1/2$ an inch (1.25cm) apart diagonally across the pastry. Quickly run the edge of a knife across the chocolate lines at $1/2$ inch intervals before the chocolate dries. The knife will pull a thin line of the chocolate along with it creating a crisscross pattern. Refrigerate the pastry and allow the egg white and chocolate to set. Cut the pastry into slices with a bread knife.

Marzipan Pears in Pâté Sucré Serves 6

This sweet pastry is ideal for making continental patisseries. Use butter that is soft, and this pastry holds its shape when handled with care. It shrinks very little and does not spread during baking and comes out thin and crisp. With this recipe you will have a little more pastry than required, this will allow for rolling the top part of the pastry case a little larger for easy handling and trimming. Bake the leftover pastry as biscuits.

8 oz (225 g) plain flour
4 oz (110 g) caster sugar
1/4 teaspoon finely crushed/milled ground cardamom
4 oz (110 g) butter at room temperature, cubed
4 egg yolks
3 small comice pears, firm
3 oz (75 g) marzipan (health food stores have a less sweet version)

Sift the flour onto a work surface. Make a large well in the centre of the flour and place the sugar, cardamom, butter and egg yolks in it. Pinch the sugar, cardamom, butter and egg yolk mixture with the fingertips of one hand until it resembles moist scrambled eggs Gradually work the mixture into the flour, using your fingers. When all the flour has been incorporated, form into a ball and knead lightly until smooth. Wrap the pastry in foil and leave to rest in the fridge for at least 30 minutes. The pastry can be made a day before but always allow it to return to room temperature before using.

Prepare the pears by cutting them into halves. Scoop out a little of each, making sure to leave the body of the pear intact. Mop up excess juice from the inside and fill with marzipan. Grease a 9 inch (23cm) round shallow sandwich cake tin and line with greaseproof paper.

Take a little less than half of the pastry and roll it out on a well-dusted work surface. Lift it with the rolling pin and gently place in the tin. Trim the excess pastry leaving enough to cover the bottom. If the pastry breaks in places, gently press it in place. Place the pears on the pastry, with the cut sides down and leaving some clearance at the rim of the tin. Roll out the remainder of the pastry to a size larger than the tin and place it over the tin. Trim, leaving enough to tuck and press over the bottom layer. With a sharp knife cut little eye shapes off the pastry right above the humps of the pears. Brush lightly with a little egg yolk. Bake in a preheated oven at 180°c (350°f) for about 30 - 35 minutes until the pastry is cooked and has turned light brown. Allow to cool in the tin and then run a knife around the tin and gently turn out. Alternately, cut into six segments and lift each out of the tin.

Fruit Salad with Rosewater & Yoghurt

Serves 4

Rosewater is an extract from a particular variety of wild roses. It has a lovely scent and subtle flavour and when used with discretion can give a very distinct flavour to the dish. It is used particularly in the Middle East for sweet dishes. Rosewater can be very easily purchased from an oriental grocery, but do check the expiry date as the flavour and scent will fade. Some chemists and health food stores do sell it, but ask for the concentrated cooking variety.

> any seasonal fresh fruit may be used
> 8 oz (225 g) fresh strawberries, washed and cut
> 4 ripe kiwi fruit, peeled and diced
> 10 kumquats cut into halves and seeded
> or 1 small orange, peeled and diced
> 8 oz (225 g) black grapes cut in half
> 1 ripe banana, halved and diced
> 1lb 4 oz (560g) thick Greek yoghurt
> 4 oz (110 g) honey, preferably acacia
> A few drops to 1 teaspoon rosewater
> (vary amount according to the strength of flavour)

In a large bowl mix the yoghurt and honey until the honey has dissolved and then add the fruit. To preserve the scent of the rosewater, add it just before serving.

Prune Mousse with Yoghurt

Serves 6 - 8

Prunes are the dried fruit of the plum. When dried their sugars become concentrated. For this reason no sugar is added in this recipe - add a little honey if required. Prunes may be replaced with dried figs or dried apricots.

> 8 oz (225 g) stoned prunes
> or 10 oz (275 g) with stones
> 1lb 2 oz (500g) thick yoghurt
> 1 tablespoon lemon juice, optional
> A little honey if required
> 2 oz (50 g) roasted almond flakes

In a medium size pan, cover the prunes with water and cook for about 10 minutes until the prunes are very soft. Allow them to cool and remove the stones if necessary. Blend the prunes with the yoghurt until very smooth. Add lemon juice and honey if desired. Serve with lightly toasted almond flakes sprinkled on top.

Almond Cake

Greeks being the first cultivators of Almonds, The Romans called them the Greek nuts. There are two varieties of Almonds; one sweet and one bitter which makes them inedible and so are used for almond oil and volatile substances. The greenish covering in which the useful seed is enclosed is leathery and when the fruit is ripe this covering opens and the stone falls out. Botanically, almonds are a fruit; the small tree is closely related to the peach. They are a very good source of plant protein, B vitamins, essential minerals, unsaturated fats and fibre. Almonds are a complete protein, containing all eight of the essential amino acids and also many other important nutrients.

This cake does not use any flour and a small piece will go a long way. The almonds combined with lemon juice give a teasing taste to the buds. It has a very delicate texture and the cake literally melts in your mouth. It is simple to make and if stored in an airtight container will keep well in the fridge for a week and for much longer in the freezer. Now that the recipe appears in print, no one will have to be convinced that this cake doesn't use any flour!

5 oz (125g) caster sugar
2 large eggs separated
3 oz (75g) margarine at room temperature
6 oz (150g) ground almond
1 teaspoon vanilla essence
juice of one large lemon
1 tablespoon icing sugar, optional

In a large bowl, beat with a spoon the margarine and sugar, until the sugar is dissolved and the mixture looks creamy. Add egg yolks and beat further until it is completely incorporated. Add the ground almond, vanilla essence and the lemon juice and mix well. Beat the egg whites with a pinch of salt until stiff. Fold them gently into the mixture. Oil a 9 inch (23cm) round shallow sandwich baking tin, and line it with a greaseproof paper. Pour in the mixture and bake in a preheated oven at 180°c (350°f) for approximately 15 -20 minutes until golden brown. Leave it in the tin for about 5 minutes and run a knife around the tin, turn it upside down on a wire rack and pull off the paper very gently. When cooled, dust it with icing sugar.

Apple Crumble

This simple pudding has always been very popular with the students. So easy to make, anyone can do it. Brockwood Park has many apple trees, therefore a plentiful supply of apples in season and always a store of fruit in the freezer, so the main ingredient is readily available.

crumble

2 lb (900 g) cooking apples

sugar to taste

1 level teaspoon powdered cinnamon

a pinch of cloves

2 tablespoons of water

Peel core and slice the apples and place in a saucepan with the water, sugar, cinnamon and cloves and cook gently until soft. Spoon in the mixture into a shallow pie dish approximately 9 inches (23cm) diameter.

crumble topping

6 oz (175g) whole wheat flour

2 oz (50g) rolled oats

3 oz (75g) butter at room temperature

3 oz (75g) soft brown sugar

a few sunflower seeds

Place the flour in a mixing bowl, add the butter and oats and rub together using your finger tips until a crumbly mixture results, stir in the sugar. Sprinkle the crumble mix on top of the apple spreading it evenly. Sprinkle top with a few sunflower seeds and bake at 180°c (350°f) for 30 - 40 minutes until golden.

Krishnamurti in the lunch tent at the
Brockwood gatherings, 1970's.

Michael Krohnen

"Cooking is an art, like writing a piece of music. It requires the capacity to harmonise and unify various textures and substances, oils and perfumes. It starts with the simple mixing and blending of the ingredients (and goes) all the way to the visual presentation".

Michael developed his flair for preparing wonderful vegetarian meals during a long and colourful period cooking for Krishnamurti and his guests in Ojai, California. From 1975 to 1986, Michael went from knowing next to nothing about cookery to being a superb chef de cuisine. "There was great freedom in starting from scratch, from absolute zero. I realised that I didn't know a thing and, therefore, was free to discover and find out for myself". This didn't mean that he didn't have help; some on-the-job training at the hands of Alan and Helen Hooker helped immensely, Alan being a renowned local restaurateur and cookery book author and a trustee of the Krishnamurti Foundation of America. But however he did it, Michael can be relied upon to come up with something special for the table whenever he is called upon to do so - which is often.

Alan and Helen Hooker with friends in the very early days.

MICHAEL KROHNEN'S
DINNER ONE

Serves 4 - 6

Greek Indian Cucumber Salad

Steamed Quinoa

Zucchini Quiche

Carrot and Poppyseed Cake

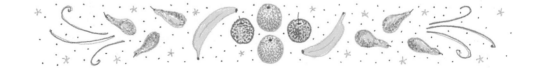

Greek Indian Cucumber Salad

    2 - 3 medium size cucumbers, peeled
    8 fl oz (225ml) (1 cup) yoghurt or sour cream
    juice of one lemon
    1 tablespoon honey
    1/4 teaspoon cumin powder
    1 clove garlic, minced
    2 tablespoons cilantro (coriander) leaves chopped fine
    salt
    pepper
    green lettuce leaves

After peeling the cucumbers, cut them lengthwise into quarters and scoop out the seeds with a spoon. Grate the remaining cucumber quarters, sprinkle them liberally with salt and place in a sieve on top of a bowl for several hours to let the water drain out. Squeeze out the remaining water just before mixing it with the spices and the yoghurt or sour cream.

Mix the lemon juice, honey and cumin powder into a smooth blend and stir into the yoghurt. Stir in the minced garlic into the grated cucumbers. Just before serving, thoroughly mix the drained cucumbers with the yoghurt mixture and the chopped cilantro leaves. Add salt and pepper according to your taste. Serve on crisp green lettuce leaves.

Steamed Quinoa

    6 1/2 oz (180g) (1 cup) quinoa grain
    16 fl oz (500ml) (2 cups) boiling water
    1/2 teaspoon salt
    1 bunch parsley, de-stemmed and chopped fine
    2 tablespoons pine nuts
    2 tablespoons raisins
    juice from one lemon
    1 tablespoon sesame oil, preferably toasted

Place the grain and the salt in a medium sized cooking pot. Pour the boiling water on top of it, cover tightly with a lid, and let simmer until all of the water is absorbed. Check with a spoon by scratching the bottom of the pot. When the grain starts to stick to the bottom, turn off the heat. Fluff and loosen the grain with a fork before mixing in the other ingredients.

Zucchini Quiche

4 medium size zucchinis, coarsely grated
2 cloves garlic, chopped fine
$1^1/2$ spanish onion, chopped fine
4 stalks celery, cubed finely
$^1/4$ teaspoon dried oregano
$^1/4$ teaspoon dill weed
1 tablespoon olive oil
1 bunch parsley, de-stemmed and chopped fine
4 eggs, thoroughly whisked
8 oz (225 g) ricotta cheese, or 5 tablespoons heavy cream
8 oz (225 g) gruyere cheese, grated fine
salt
pepper
1 tablespoon sunflower seeds

Sprinkle salt on the grated zucchini, place in a sieve on top of a bowl and let the water drain out. Before mixing with the other ingredients, firmly squeeze the remaining water from the grated zucchini.

In a frying pan, sauté the chopped garlic. Add the chopped onions and cook until lightly brown. Next add the cubed celery. Cook for another few minutes before adding the oregano and the dill weed. Add a sprinkle of salt and a dash of freshly ground pepper.

In a large mixing bowl, beat the eggs and thoroughly mix with the ricotta cheese or cream and the Gruyere. Add the drained zucchini, the fried onion/celery mixture, and the raw chopped parsley. Stir to a smooth consistency. Taste to check if sufficiently salty.

Pour the mixture into a low glass or ceramic baking pan (round or square) that has been thoroughly oiled or buttered. Smooth the top and sprinkle the sunflower seeds on it. Bake in a preheated oven at 350°f (180°c) for approx 30 - 40 minutes. The top should be lightly browned.

Carrot and Poppyseed Cake

2 eggs, thoroughly beaten
4 oz (110 g) butter, melted
5 oz (150 g) (^{2}/3 cup) sugar
^{1}/2 tablespoon vanilla extract
^{1}/2 teaspoon cinnamon
^{1}/4 teaspoon cardamon powder, freshly ground
^{1}/8 teaspoon ground cloves
^{1}/8 teaspoon ground nutmeg, freshly ground
1 tablespoon poppy seeds
4 fl oz (125ml) (^{1}/2 cup) yoghurt
5 oz (150 g) (1 cup) flour
^{1}/4 teaspoon baking powder
^{1}/4 teaspoon salt
5 oz (150 g) (1 cup) finely grated carrots
2^1/2 oz (60 g) (^{1}/2 cup) raisins
the peel of one orange, grated
1 tablespoon orange liqueur, cointreau or grand marnier

Mix together in a large bowl, butter, sugar and spices. Stir to a smooth consistency and add the yoghurt. Sift in the flour, salt and baking powder mixture.

Separately, in a cuisinart or other type of kitchen blender, blend the carrots, raisins, orange peel and orange liqueur. Once you have a gooey mass, thoroughly stir into the egg/flour mixture. Pour the mixture into an oiled baking pan. Bake in a preheated oven at 350°f (180°c) for 35 - 45 minutes. Test it with a toothpick: if it comes out clean it's done.

MICHAEL KROHNEN'S
DINNER TWO

Serves 4 - 6

Fresh Carrot and Ginger Salad

Saffron Basmati Rice

Eggplant Parmesan

Tomato Sauce

Apricot Cream

Fresh Carrot and Ginger Salad

1 lb (450g) organic carrots, peeled and grated medium fine
juice of 2 lemons or limes
1^1/$_2$ tablespoons honey
pinch of salt
^{1}/$_2$ inch bulb of fresh ginger root, skinned
^{1}/$_2$ cup of currants
1 small green bell pepper
twigs of parsley
several slices of lemon

Immediately after grating the carrots, pour the mixture of lemon juice and honey over them, stirring thoroughly to prevent the carrots from oxidising. Mix in the other ingredients and present in a bowl. Embellish with grated fine sprigs of parsley and half slices of lemon.

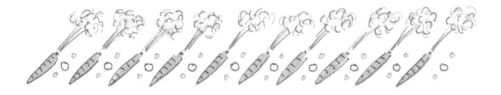

Saffron Basmati Rice

12 oz (350g) (2 cups) white or brown rice, thoroughly rinsed and dried
1 teaspoon salt, or to taste
^{1}/$_4$ teaspoon saffron powder

Place in a pot, preferably stainless steel, add salt and saffron. Pour 4 cups boiling water over the rice. Cover with tight lid. Lower heat to simmering and cook until all water is absorbed, approx 20 minutes for white, 40 minutes for brown rice. Fluff with fork. Garnish with toasted almonds or cashew nuts.

Eggplant Parmesan

2 - 3 medium to large eggplants
olive oil
cinnamon powder
herb salt
tomato sauce, see next page
Parmesan cheese, freshly grated, approx 1 oz (25 g)
1lb 4 oz mozzarella cheese
1/2 bunch parsley, finely chopped

Wash eggplant. Cut off end portions, cut lengthwise into 3/4 inch slices after peeling off skin of first and last slices. Brush lightly with olive oil and place on oiled baking sheet. Grill on both sides until golden brown. Oil Pyrex baking pan 8 inch x 13 inch and 2 inches deep. Cover bottom with a bit of sauce, then cut grilled eggplant slices into 2 inch sections and place on top of sauce, covering bottom of pan. Sprinkle a bit of herb salt and cinnamon powder over the eggplant, then top with thinly sliced mozzarella cheese. Cover with thin layer of tomato sauce. Repeat process once or twice (depending on the depth of pan and being careful to leave 1/2 inch top portion of pan free). End with layer of tomato sauce and sprinkle parmesan cheese on top. Bake for 40 minutes at 375°f (190°c). Allow to cool and settle for 10 minutes before serving. Garnish with finely chopped parsley.

Tomato Sauce

4 cloves of garlic, minced
olive oil, 3 tablespoons
1 medium onion, spanish
1^1/2 lbs (675 g) ripe roma tomatoes, peeled, sliced and cubed
5 tablespoons tomato concentrate
1^1/2 teaspoon sugar, any kind
1 small bunch basil, cut fine
^{1}/4 teaspoon oregano, dried
salt and pepper to taste
1 bay leaf
1^1/2 teaspoon cornstarch

In a medium sized saucepan heat the olive oil on a medium heat, add garlic. Sauté until light brown. Add onion and stir until light brown, then add tomatoes. Cook for about 10 - 15 minutes stirring frequently. Add tomato concentrate and dissolve in sauce. Now add sugar, basil, oregano, salt and freshly ground pepper and one bay leaf. Cover. Turn heat to simmer and allow to cook for about 1/2 hour, stirring occasionally, especially the bottom part.

This sauce, especially for the eggplant parmesan recipe should not be too watery. If too liquid, dissolve 1^1/2 tablespoon cornstarch in ^{1}/4 cup of water and stir into sauce at medium to high heat. This sauce is also good with pasta and other dishes.

Apricot Cream

1 lb (450 g) dried apricots
^{1}/2 pt (300ml) cream or yoghurt
1^1/2 tablespoons vanilla extract
2 oz (50g) (^{1}/4 cup) maple syrup, honey or sugar
dash of salt
2 tablespoons grand marnier or cointreau or other orange liqueur

Place dried apricots in a bowl and cover with boiling water. Allow to soak for 1 - 2 hours. Add more water if it's all absorbed. Use a kitchen aid or cuisinart to blend the softened apricots, probably in three batches, adding appropriate amount of the soaking water and the other ingredients. Blend until thick, smooth and creamy. Serve in dessert bowl with a garnish of sour cream and one of the reserved apricot halves.

MICHAEL KROHNEN'S
DINNER THREE

Serves 4 - 6

Cumin Baked Potatoes

Crustless Spinach Quiche
(à Trois Fromages)

Vegetable Provençale

Couscous Taboule

Persimmon Cream

Cumin Baked Potatoes

    5 regular baking potatoes, scrubbed and cut in half
    1 tablespoon of sunflower seed or corn oil
    1 1/2 tablespoons of cumin or caraway seeds

Lightly brush the cleaned potato halves with oil and roll them in the cumin seeds, taking care that they are not too densely covered with the seeds. Place them on an oiled baking sheet and bake them at 375°f (190°c) for 35 minutes, testing with a fork to see if they are done.

Crustless Spinach Quiche (à Trois Fromages)

    4 bunches of spinach, washed, steamed and chopped fine or 2 small
    packets of frozen spinach, defrosted
    1 bunch parsley, chopped fine
    5 eggs, beaten
    8 oz (225g) fresh goat cheese, preferably French chevre
    8 oz (225g) gruyère cheese, grated fine
    4 oz (110g) parmesan cheese, freshly grated
    1/4 teaspoon freshly ground nutmeg
    1/4 teaspoon tarragon, ground fine
    1/4 teaspoon dill
    several rounds of freshly ground pepper
    salt according to taste

After steaming spinach, chop finely and place into sieve or colander squeezing out all excess liquid. Beat the eggs in a bowl and thoroughly blend in the three cheeses and condiments. And then add the chopped spinach and parsley. Bake in the oven at 350°f (180°c) degrees for approx 30 - 40 minutes until firm. Don't overcook. The quiche should still have some firm moistness.

Vegetable Provençale

5 medium sized zucchini, washed and cut into ¼ inch rounds
8 oz (225 g)white mushrooms, cleaned and sliced
4 red and green bell peppers, cut into thin strips
rosemary
basil
oregano
salt and pepper to taste
a little olive oil
8 fl oz (250ml) (1 cup) tomato sauce, see page 123

Heat a non-stick frying pan. Place the sliced mushrooms in without any oil, just covering the surface of the pan so that each mushroom slice will be browned individually and can be flipped over with a wooden spoon. Once they are brown on either side, and the water is drawn out, sprinkle just a bit of rosemary (either dry or fresh) over them. Add salt and freshly ground pepper, and place them on the bottom of serving dish. It may take two or three batches to fry all of them. Next, do the same thing with the zucchini slices, only sprinkle basil on them at the end and a few dashes of olive oil. Take care not to overcook them. They should still be firm. Place them on top of the layer of mushrooms. Next fry the strips of bell pepper in the same way, sprinkling oregano and a dash of olive oil on them. Place them on top of the zucchini. Now take the tomato sauce and put dabs of it on top of the vegetables. Briefly re-heat the dish with the vegetables before serving.

Couscous Taboule

6½ oz (180g) (1 cup) couscous or bulghur wheat
1 teaspoon salt
2 tablespoons olive oil
2 tablespoons of lemon juice
2 bunches fresh parsley, stemmed and chopped very fine
1 bunch fresh mint, stemmed and chopped very fine
1 bunch green spring onions, chopped fine
4 tablespoons each of currants and pine nuts
2 tablespoons capers
8 sun dried tomato halves, preferably cured in olive oil, chopped fine

Place the couscous and salt in a bowl and cover with boiling water. Let stand until the grain has absorbed the water, about 20 minutes, then fluff it up with a fork, carefully separating individual clusters. Now add all the other ingredients. Let it stand for ½ to 1 hour prior to serving.

Persimmon Cream

4 ripe persimmons, fresh or frozen
$^1/_2$ pt (300ml) whipping cream
1$^1/_2$ teaspoon vanilla extract

After removing skin and bottom end of persimmons, place them in a blender together with the other ingredients. Blend thoroughly and place in serving bowls.

Note: Persimmons are quite seasonal. Once ripened they lend themselves to being frozen and kept wrapped in aluminum foil or in a tight container for up to a year in the freezer compartment.

The Krishnamurti Centre dining room.

MICHAEL KROHNEN'S
DINNER FOUR

Serves 4 - 6

Greek Salad

Wild Rice à la Grecque

Mushroom Sauce

Broccoli with Olive Sauce

Strawberries with Ginger Cream Sauce

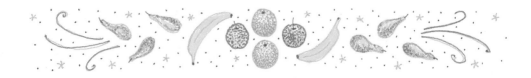

Greek Salad

1 lb (450 g) roma tomatoes, seeded and cut into $1/8$'s
3 bell peppers, yellow, green and red if possible, seeded and
cut into $1/2$ inch squares
1 cucumber peeled, seeded, quartered lengthwise and cut into $1/2$ inch sections
1 bunch spring onions, cleaned and cut fine
1 clove garlic cut fine
jar or can of black olives, preferably kalamata type, watch for stones
l small bunch fresh basil, cut fine
2 fl oz (55ml) ($1/4$ cup) olive oil
juice of 1 lemon
dash of balsamic vinegar
salt and freshly ground pepper to taste
8 oz (225 g) of feta cheese, cubed
$1/4$ bunch parsley chopped fine for garnish

Mix all the ingredients except olive oil, lemon juice, vinegar, parsley and feta cheese. Place in a flat serving bowl. Shortly before serving, sprinkle on the olive oil, lemon juice and balsamic vinegar. Place the cubed feta cheese evenly on top of the mixture and embellish with chopped parsley.

Wild Rice à la Grecque

$6^{1}/2$ oz (180g) (1 cup) wild rice, rinsed
1 tablespoon toasted sesame oil or olive oil
1 cube vegetarian bouillon soup concentrate
2 tablespoons each of the following: pine nuts, currants, capers
3 sundried tomatoes preserved in olive oil cut into small pieces
juice of $1/2$ lemon
$1/2$ bunch parsley for garnish, cut fine

Place rice in stainless steel pot (or ceramic or pyrex). Pour 3 cups of boiling water over it, together with the bouillon cube. Lower heat to simmering and cover tightly with lid. Stir occasionally for approximately $1/2$ hour. The grains should burst open and soft when done. Stir the currants, capers, pine nuts and sundried tomatoes into the rice, together with the sesame oil and lemon juice. Sprinkle the chopped parsley on top before serving.

Mushroom Sauce

1$\frac{1}{2}$ lbs (675 g) white mushrooms, washed, trimmed and sliced
1 tablespoon olive oil
1 dab of butter
1 quart of $\frac{1}{2}$ milk & $\frac{1}{2}$ cream brought to the boil
1 bay leaf
2 tablespoons corn starch
$\frac{1}{2}$ teaspoon rosemary, fresh or dried cut fine
$\frac{1}{4}$ teaspoon sage, powdered
2 teaspoon marmite
several rounds of freshly ground pepper
salt according to taste

Heat oil and butter in non-stick pan. Add sliced mushrooms and cook at medium high heat, stirring occasionally until water is drawn out of mushrooms. Add rosemary, sage, marmite and freshly ground pepper.

In a separate pan, bring to the boil the milk/cream mixture with the bay leaf, but put aside $\frac{1}{4}$ cup of the cold milk/cream mixture. Gradually add the heated milk/cream mixture to the other ingredients, stirring regularly. Let simmer for 20 minutes. Dissolve corn starch in cold milk and stir it into the mushroom mixture. When the sauce has the desired consistency, taste it and add salt if necessary. Serve over rice.

Broccoli with Olive Sauce

1$\frac{1}{2}$ lbs (675 g) broccoli tops and short stems
salt
4 fl oz (125ml) ($\frac{1}{2}$ cup) olive oil
1 small can of finely chopped black olives
1 small jar of capers, chopped fine
4 - 5 tablespoons of smoked "bakon" yeast

Wash and trim broccoli into inch-size florets. Peel stem portions and cut into $\frac{1}{2}$ inch cubes. Bring water and salt to boil in large pan and add broccoli. Be careful not to overcook the broccoli, just leave it in the boiling water for a few minutes.

Meanwhile in a separate saucepan, briefly heat olive oil just so it's room temperature, then stir in the "bakon" yeast with a wire whisk until the mixture has a smooth consistency. Add the chopped olives and the chopped capers and stir everything together. Place small amounts of this sauce onto the broccoli florets before serving.

Strawberries with Ginger Cream Sauce

3 baskets (approx 1lb 8 oz) of ripe strawberries
1 pint sour cream
1 jar of ginger preserve, preferably "Keiller" Dundee brand
in white ceramic jar
several sprigs of fresh mint

Wash and hull strawberries and divide into individual serving bowls. Mix sour cream and $1/4$ ginger preserve or jam and spoon over strawberries. Garnish with sprigs of fresh mint.

Derek Hook

Derek Hook is a restaurateur in the English Lake District, running the popular vegetarian restaurant, Zeffirelli's. He lives at Yewfield, a guest house, with Gary Primrose and Christina West who were long time staff members at Brockwood.

A trustee of the Foundation, he still enjoys cooking and has been a guest cook at the Centre on many occasions.

For the Brockwood Cookbook, I thought it would be useful to have two meals that can be done quite quickly, that are easy to make and taste great, and one dish that is a little more involved for a special occasion. And, as we often get asked here at Yewfield for Gary's bread recipe, here it is.

Yewfield bread

SPECIAL OCCASION MENU

Serves 4-6

Parmesan Polenta with a Black Olive & Chili Tapenade

Hazelnut & Mushroom Roast with a Red Pepper Sauce

Rosemary Roast Potatoes

Poached Apricots with Ginger & Lemon

Parmesan Polenta with Black Olive Tapenade

parmesan polenta
9oz (250g) quick cook polenta
3 tablespoons olive oil
2oz (50g) butter
2$^{1}/_{2}$ oz (60g) fresh grated parmesan
1 tablespoon dried sage
salt and black pepper

Follow quick cook polenta instructions adding salt as required. When almost complete
and bubbling stir in the olive oil, butter, sage and parmesan grinding in fresh black
pepper. Spread the mixture into an oiled one inch deep, 10 inch diameter round dish and
leave to stand for 20 minutes. Slice the polenta into 8 wedges and grill for 5 minutes or
until slightly brown on top.

tapenade
4oz (110g) of good quality stoned black olives,
preserved in oil not vinegar
2 tablespoons of olive oil
a few sprigs of fresh coriander
$^{1}/_{2}$ lime or lemon juiced
2 cloves of garlic
1 fresh chili

Blend the olives, olive oil, red chili in a food processor. Add the juice of one lime and
chop the fresh coriander into the tapenade mixture.

The Parmesan Polenta makes a delicious starter served grilled with a little fresh parmesan
and tossed leaves.

Mushroom and Hazelnut Roast (Pâté) Serves ????

mushroom & hazelnut roast
olive oil
1lb (450g) button mushrooms, chopped small
1 medium onion
4 cloves garlic
8oz (230g) roasted hazelnuts, ground
7oz (200g) whole-wheat breadcrumbs
2 tablespoons (3oz, 80g approx) marmite or vecon
2 tablespoons mixed herbs
fresh black pepper
2 free range eggs

Chop the onions and garlic finely. Put the oil on a high heat in a large saucepan. When hot add the onion and garlic and leave to sizzle for a few minutes. Then add the chopped mushrooms, stir until cooked down. Add the marmite, mixing in well. Then add the herbs and plenty of fresh black pepper. Take off the heat, whisk the eggs and stir them into the mixture. Add the ground roasted hazelnuts and breadcrumbs. Put the complete mixture into an oiled bread tin or baking dish and roast in the oven at 190°c (375°f) for 30-40 minutes until brown on top.

red pepper sauce
2 red peppers
1 onion
2 cloves garlic
6 good fresh Italian tomatoes, peeled and chopped
5 leaves of fresh basil
olive oil
black pepper and salt

In a saucepan add a little olive oil. When hot add the chopped onion and garlic followed by the peppers chopped small. Cook until soft then add the chopped tomatoes. Simmer for approx 20 minutes. Grind the black pepper and add the salt and basil and liquidise with the blender. A nice touch is to squeeze a little lemon into the sauce just before serving.

Serve the sauce not completely over the roast, with roast potatoes, next page, on the side with either buttered sprouts or steamed brocolli and a little apple sauce.

Rosemary Roast Potatoes

6 - 8 roasting potatoes
3 sprigs of rosemary
olive oil
salt and black pepper

Cut the potatoes into nice sized roasting pieces. Parboil in salted water until not quite soft. Drain and save the water for stock. Put the potatoes in a roasting dish, sprinkle with olive oil and then sprinkle with the rosemary leaves on top. Add black pepper and salt to taste. Roast in hot oven until golden brown.

Poached Apricots with Pear, Ginger & Lemon

24 fl oz (750ml) (3 cups) water
7 oz (200g) (1 cup) sugar
$1^1/2$ oz (40g) peeled fresh ginger, fine threads
7 ozs (200g) apricots, dried
peel of one lemon, thin slices
crisp pear peeled and thinly cut

Combine water and sugar and bring to boil. Add the ginger and simmer for 5 minutes. Add the dried apricots and lemon peel. Lower the heat and cook for abut 20 minutes until the apricots are soft but not breaking up. Take out the apricots with a slotted spoon and put into a dish. Simmer the remaining syrup until bubbles appear (5-6 minutes). Add the slices of pear to the apricots and pour the syrup over the dish. Leave to chill in the fridge. When cold put into individual dishes and top with fromage frais, a sprig of fresh mint and a few toasted almond flakes.

Pasta Zucchini con Pomodora

My favourite style of cooking is Italian and the knack of good Italian cooking comes down to using the very best ingredients. You need excellent olive oil for finishing, and good cooking olive oil, together with those lovely Roma tomatoes, fresh herbs including basil, oregano and rosemary and, of course, Italian cheeses.

This dish is simple to make and is one I make at Yewfield often. We like the chilli but for those who don't like things too spicy, they can be omitted.

2lb (900g) Roma tomatoes or vine tomatoes (or Italian tinned if not available) *(To skin tomatoes, cut out the seed and make a cross on the top. Place in boiling water for a minute or so. The skin will just come off. Then pulp the tomato with a fork.)*
1 medium onion, chopped small
1 small-medium red and green pepper, diced
2 nice courgettes, about 14oz (400g) *(To prepare slice courgettes down from top to bottom then again to make four quarters, then chop along)*
3 little dried chillies (optional) chopped small
3 large good sized cloves of garlic, chopped small
4 tablespoons cooking olive oil
2 tablespoons best virgin olive oil, to finish
Fresh basil and fresh parsley
A good tablespoon white flour
1 teaspoon of salt, to taste and ample fresh black pepper
A few good black olives in oil (not vinegar)
Fresh grated Parmesan
The juice of one lemon
1 packet of pasta, not wholewheat *(allow 100g per person - penne is good)*

In a good-sized stainless steel saucepan heat 4 tablespoons of cooking olive oil. When hot add the chilli and garlic and sizzle for a minute. Then add the onion, keeping the flame hot. One minute later, add the chopped peppers, after another minute add the courgettes. These won't take long to cook, maybe 2-3 minutes. When the vegetables look as if they are cooking, sprinkle in the flour, stirring well. Turn down the heat a little and stir in the chopped tomatoes. This will now turn into a sauce. Chop the parsley and basil saving a few basil leaves for the top and add to the sauce. Leave gently simmering for 5 minutes, stirring occasionally to prevent it sticking, then add 2-3 tablespoons of your best virgin olive oil to the sauce which should now have a smooth sheen and is ready to serve. At this time, put in the olives and juice from the squeezed lemon. Meanwhile, boil the water for pasta as indicated on the packet. Cook to al dente, drain and stir in some good olive oil before serving. Portion the pasta into nice sized pasta bowls and top with a little of the sauce. Serve with fresh Parmesan and rocket leaves on top. A few pine nuts would be nice. We have this dish accompanied by leaves from the garden and Gary's bread with rosemary.

Potato, Cheese and Vegetable Crisp *Serves 6-8*

This is a very tasty dish that's easy to make and welcome after a long walk on an autumn day.

Ingredients for the filling
4-6 good sized potatoes

1 head of a firm cauliflower, approx 1lb 2oz (500g) cut into small florets

2 leeks (chopped small) approx 12oz (350g) prepared

2 carrots, chopped, approx 8oz (225g)

2 courgettes, approx 8oz (225g)

4 oz (110g) mushrooms, sliced

2 tablespoons dried mixed herbs (if you have fresh ones,
use a good handful chopped small)

1 x 450g tin of chopped tomatoes

4 cloves of garlic

$1^1/_2$ oz (40g) of vecon or vegetable bouillon

1 heaped tablespoon of white or brown flour

Olive oil and black pepper

Stock from the potatoes

Cheese Sauce
$3/_4$ pint (425ml) of milk

6 oz (175g) grated cheddar

$1/_2$ medium onion chopped small

10 leaves of garden mint, chopped small

4 tablespoons of olive oil

salt and black pepper

First clean and slice the potatoes quartered in rounds or thereabouts and place into a pan of salted water and put onto the heat. They should be parboiled, not too soft.

While the potatoes are cooking, you can make a start on the vegetable base. In a heavy based stainless steel saucepan heat 4-5 tablespoons of olive oil. When hot add the garlic, then the leeks. Sizzle a little before adding the following ingredients, in the order indicated, cooking them over a high heat: first the carrots, than one minute later the cauliflower, then a further minute later the courgettes and lastly the chopped mushrooms. Stir over the heat until the cauliflower looks cooked but still a little crunchy, then stir in the heaped tablespoon of flour. This will help to make the liquid hold together. Now add the tomatoes and stir in the herbs. In a bowl with six tablespoons of stock blend the vecon or vegetable bouillon and add to the vegetables. Give a good few twists of fresh ground pepper and if the vegetable base looks a little dry, you can add a little more stock. Place the vegetables in a baking dish with the potatoes placed to cover the top and baste with a little olive oil and a sprinkling of salt and put in a hot oven, 220°c until the potatoes begin to turn a little brown, about 15 minutes.

While the bake is in the oven, make the cheese sauce. In a stainless steel pan heat 4 tablespoons of olive oil and when hot throw in the chopped onion and sizzle a little. Now stir into the onion the tablespoons of white flour and let the onions take up the flour. Turn down the heat and slowly stir in the milk making a creamy sauce, stirring all the time. Add the cheese, salt and the chopped mint and bring to bubble.

Take the vegetable and potato bake out of the oven and pour on the cheese sauce. Replace in the oven for 10 minutes and it will soon look ready. This dish is best served in one of those pasta bowls with a nice crunchy salad on the side.

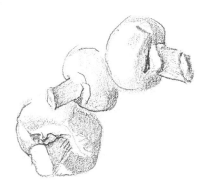

Fruit Snow   *Serves 6-8*

Here is a simple dessert that is very easy to prepare and tastes delicious.

> 6 oz (175g)chopped dried apricots
> 2 bananas cut into little rounds
> 2 pears, peeled, de-pipped and chopped
> 9 oz (250g) fresh or frozen raspberries
> A jar of bilberries in juice or syrup (470g in total)
> A lemon, grated and juiced
> 5 oz (150g) desiccated coconut

Put the chopped apricots with the juice of the bilberries and the lemon rind in a stainless steel saucepan and bring to simmer on top of the stove. Leave gently to cook for about 5 minutes than take off the heat, add the chopped pear and bananas and leave for 10 minutes. Now add the bilberries and raspberries and stir in the lemon juice. Place the fruits in a serving bowl.

Toast the dessicated coconut on top of the stove in an ungreased frying pan until a little brown, then add to the top of the prepared fruits.

This dessert is really nice served still a little warm, with running cream.

A Quick Fruit Crumble

Serves 6-8

Pear, Banana and Sultana

This crumble can be ready in 15 minutes and is delicious. You cook mostly on top of the stove and finish in a hot oven!

For the crumble topping:
5oz (150g) good muesli mix with dried fruits and nuts (not peanuts)
4oz (110g) butter
2oz (50g) demerara sugar
2oz (50g) flour (white or wholewheat)

For the fruit filling:
4 pears (Conference pears are good)
3 bananas
3oz (75g) dried sultanas
6fl oz (180ml) orange juice
Or you can use any fruit combination of similar quantities:
Apple and blackberries
Gooseberries
Rhubarb, apricot and stem ginger
basically, whatever seasonal fruits are in abundance.

As this is all done rather quickly it is best to first turn on the oven to 220°c (425°f)

Prepare the fruit, chop and wash the pears, taking out the pips, chop the banana and put all the fruits in a pan with the orange juice and place over a light heat on the stove. Leave the fruit to cook whilst preparing the crumble topping.

In a large heavy frying pan or wok, melt the butter. When sizzling stir in the muesli mix and cook for approximately two minutes. Add the sugar, then lastly the flour which you will find turns the mixture into a crumbly combination. By this time, the fruits can be put into a baking dish. Add the crumble topping, place in the now hot oven and within a few minutes it should start to bubble and will have turned a nice golden brown.

Serve it with a little cream or yoghurt.

Yewfield Bread

4lbs (1.8kg) flour - a combination of strong organic bread flours
(We use: 2lbs (900g) wholemeal flour, 1lb (450g) spelt flour
and 1lb (450g) white flour)
3 level teaspoons quick acting dried yeast
4 teaspoons sea salt
$^1/2$ oz (10g) sesame seeds
$^3/4$ oz (20g) sunflower seeds
4 teaspoons organic sunflower oil plus a little for brushing the loaves
approx $2^1/2$ pints (1.5 litres) hand hot water
4 x 2lb (900g) loaf tins

Mix all dry ingredients thoroughly in a large bowl including the yeast. Make a well in the middle and add approximately $2^1/2$ pints (1.5 litres) hand hot water, folding the flour into the water and then mixing well. The dough should not too stiff.

Turn the dough out on to a well floured board and knead for at least 5 minutes until the dough springs back when depressed by your thumb. Put the kneaded dough back in the mixing bowl and cover with a tea towel moistened with hot water. Put in a warm place until the dough has risen to double size. Depending on the temperature this will take from 1 to $1^1/2$ hours.

Meanwhile generously oil the loaf tins with 1 tsp of oil per tin and put them in a warm place. When the dough has risen to twice its original size turn it out onto a well floured board and divide into four pieces, each approximately 1lb 10oz (800g). Shape each loaf by tucking in the edges underneath and leaving a smooth surface on top before putting them in the tins. Brush the surface of the loaves with oil to prevent the crust drying out during the rising process. Allow to rise for a further $^1/2$ hour to 1 hour or until double in size.

Preheat the oven to 200°c (400°f), placing a tray of hot water in the bottom to evaporate as the loaves bake. The moister air in the oven helps develop the crust. Put the loaves in the oven when risen and spray with water using a hand sprayer. Bake for 25 minutes then turn the loaves out of the tins directly onto the oven racks and spray them with water again. Bake for a further 3 minutes to further develop the crust. Remove loaves from the oven and cool them on a rack.

Tips

Yeast: normally bread recipes call for 1 tsp of dried yeast per pound (450g) flour but this recipe uses less. The dough takes longer to rise but in the process of a longer rising a less yeasty, more complex flavour develops as well as a chewier "crumb" - the term that bakers use for the texture of a loaf.

Temperature: to follow the timings in the recipe keep all the ingredients warm. The dough will take longer to rise if cooled but still makes a good loaf.

Conversion Tables

These are approximate (rounded up or down)

Weights

½ oz	10g
1 oz	25g
1½ oz	40g
2 oz	50g
2½ oz	60g
3 oz	75g
4 oz	110g
5 oz	150g
6 oz	175g
7 oz	200g
8 oz	225g
9 oz	250g
10 oz	275g
12 oz	350g
1lb	450g

Volume

2 fl oz	55ml
3 oz	75ml
5 (¼ pint)	150ml
½ pint	300ml
¾ pint	450ml
1 pint	570ml
1 ¾ pint	1 litre

Oven Temperatures

	°C	°F	Gas Mark
Very Low	110-130	225-250	¼ - ½
Cool	150	300	2
Warm	170	325	3
Moderate	180	350	4
Fairly Hot	200	400	6
Hot	220	425	7
Very Hot	240	475	9

Cup Equivalents

1 cup – 8 fl oz (US), 250 ml (Metric)

1 cup of soft brown sugar – 6 oz (170g)

1 cup of demerara sugar – 7oz (200g)

1 cup flour – 5 oz (140g)

1 cup oats – 3 oz (85g)

1 cup nuts – 4-5 oz (110-140g)

1 cup dried fruit – 5oz (140g)

1 cup dried beans – 6½ oz (180g)

1 cup white rice (dry) – 6oz (170g)

1 cup brown rice (dry) – 6½ oz (180g)

1 cup seeds (eg: sunflower/sesame) – 4½ oz (125g)

1 cup lentils (dry) – 6oz (170g)

1 cup grated cheese – 4oz (110g)

1 cup diced onion, potato or carrots – about 5oz (140g)

Index

Soups

Beetroot Soup 14
Carrot Soup 15
Carrot and Leek Soup 14
Celeriac Soup 15
Chickpea with Rosemary Soup 16
Dahl Soup 17
Fresh Pea Soup 16
Leek Soup 17
Lentil Soup 18
Mushroom Soup 18
Pumpkin Soup 19
Split Pea Soup 20
Watercress Soup 19

Starters

Cumin Baked Potatoes 125
Fresh Carrot and Ginger Salad 121
Greek Indian Cucumber Salad 117
Greek Salad 129
Parmesan Polenta with a
Black Olive & Chili Tapenade 134
Wild Rice à la Grecque 129

Complementary Dishes

Chapati 69
Couscous Taboule 126
Cucumber Raita 71
Cumin Baked Potatoes 125
Deep Fried Pooris 70
Rosemary Roast Potatoes 136
Saffron Basmati Rice 121
Steamed Quinoa 117
Vegetable Provençale 126
Yewfield Bread 141

Pâté

Avocado Pâté (Guacamole) 75
Olive/Capers/Sundried Tomatoes Pâté .. 74
Smoke Flavoured Aubergine Pâté 73
Tofu Pâté 72

Dressings

Mayonnaise 50
Sesame Soy Dressing 51
Sweet Yellow Mayonnaise 50
Vinaigrette 50

Main Dishes

Bean Cakes 24
Butterbean Casserole 25
Butter Bean Stew 86
Butterbean or Tofu Stroganoff 26
Chickpea Curry 82
Chinese Stir Fry with Tofu
& Garlic Ginger Sauce 90
Chow Mein with Fried Tofu 88
Corn Savoury 27
Crustless Spinach Quiche
(À Trois Fromages) 125
Eggplant Parmesan 122
Filled Tomatoes 28
Four Rice with Mung Bean Sprouts 91
Handwa - Fermented Yoghurt Bake 84
Hazelnut & Mushroom Roast
with a Red Pepper Sauce 135
Indian Stir Fry 89
Kalyani Rice 29
Leek Croustade 30
Lentil Rissoles 31
Moussaka 32
Mushroom Nut Roast
with Spicy Peanut Sauce 33
Mushroom Pancakes 34
Okra 87
Pasta Zucchini con Pomodora 137
Penne Arrabbiata 94
Pesto with Fusilli, Roasted
Peppers & Aubergines 83
Potato, Cheese and Vegetable Crisp 138
Ratatouille 93
Shepherds Pie 35
Spiced Aubergine 95
Spicy Vegetables &
Chickpeas with Couscous 39
Spinach Rice Bake 38
Spinakopita 92
Split Mung Dahl (Lentil) 96
Tandoori Bean Cakes 36
Tofu with Broccoli 85
Tofu with Tarragon
and Mushroom Sauce 37
Turtle Beans with Fresh Coriander 97
Zucchini Quiche 118

Index

Pastry Dishes

Broccoli Flan 40
Carrot Flan with Potato Peanut Pastry 41
Miso Pie 42
Onion Tart 43
Spinach Pie 44
Vegetable Cobbler 45
Winter Vegetable Pie 46

Sauces

All Purpose Curry Sauce 80
All Purpose Pomarola Tomato Sauce
Versions 1 & 2 76
Broccoli with Olive Sauce 130
Mushroom Sauce 79
Mushroom Sauce 130
Pesto Sauce 78
Tomato Sauce 123

Cakes, Cookies & Desserts

Almond Cake 111
Almond Tart 54
Apple & Almond Cake 55
Apple and Nuts in Filo Pastry 107
Apple Crumble 112
Apricot Cream 123
Banana Raisin Teabread 55
Blackcurrant Cream 56
Brockwood Cookies 56
Carrot Cake 57
Carrot and Poppyseed Cake 119
Chocolate Cake 58
Chocolate Mousse
with Grand Marnier 106
Cream Caramel 99
Date and Orange Cake 60
Esme's Recipe for Wholemeal Scones 59
Fruit Salad with Rosewater & Yoghurt .. 110
Fruit Snow 139
Greek Lemon Cake 59
Mango Cream 104
Marzipan Pears in Pâté Sucree 109
Mille-Feuilles 108
Not So Naughty Cheesecake 60
Pear Cake 102
Persimmon Cream 127
Pineapple Meringue 61

Poached Apricots with
Ginger & Lemon 136
Prune Mousse with Yoghurt 110
Quick Fruit Crumble 140
Rosewater & Yoghurt Cake 101
Saffron Rice Pudding 100
Shikhand 103
Strawberries with Ginger
Cream Sauce 131
Tarte En Bande 105
Toffee Date Cake 62

Complete Dinners

Dinner One
Greek Indian Cucumber Salad 117
Steamed Quinoa 117
Zucchini Quiche 118
Carrot and Poppyseed Cake 119

Dinner Two
Fresh Carrot and Ginger Salad 121
Saffron Basmati Rice 121
Eggplant Parmesan 122
Tomato Sauce 123
Apricot Cream 123

Dinner Three
Cumin Baked Potatoes 125
Crustless Spinach Quiche
(À Trois Fromages) 125
Vegetable Provençale 126
Couscous Taboule 126
Persimmon Cream 127

Dinner Four
Greek Salad 129
Wild Rice à la Grecque 129
Mushroom Sauce 130
Broccoli with Olive Sauce 130
Strawberries with Ginger
Cream Sauce 131

Special Occasion Menu
Parmesan Polenta with a
Black Olive & Chili Tapenade 134
Hazelnut & Mushroom Roast
with a Red Pepper Sauce 135
Rosemary Roast Potatoes 136
Poached Apricots with
Ginger & Lemon 136
Yewfield Bread 141